P9-CDP-216

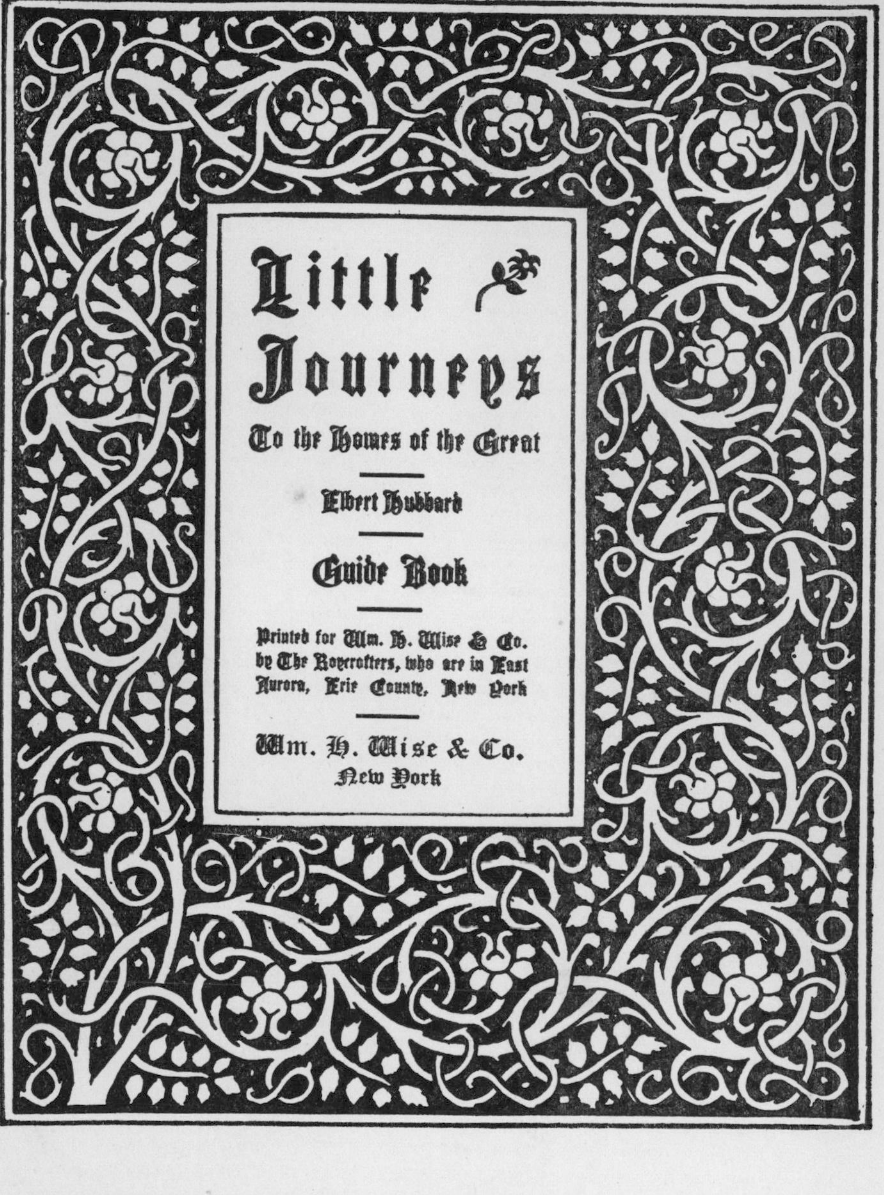

Little Journeys

To the Homes of the Great

Elbert Hubbard

Guide Book

Printed for Wm. H. Wise & Co. by The Roycrofters, who are in East Aurora, Erie County, New York

Wm. H. Wise & Co.
New York

FOREWORD

HE purpose of a guide-book is to direct you and give you your bearings. When you go into a strange city, oftentimes you are bewildered by the many things to be seen. Where shall you begin? There is so much of it, and all so wonderful! How can you take it all in?

The fourteen volumes of Elbert Hubbard's masterpiece, Little Journeys to the Homes of the Great, are like a rich walled city, of spires, cathedrals, palaces and art galleries, with winding streets and fragrant courtyards full of vivid personalities.

Wherever you turn, your eye is enriched with pictures, and your ear with music and the murmur of pleasant voices. You may wander at random and never tire. You may take half-hour visits in famous homes.

A guide-book is primarily for him who would savor all the delights of the great city. It shows you how to proceed without confusion or loss of time from one colorful quarter to another.

Here twenty-five centuries of human life have gathered their best inside the walls of a magical city. Twenty-five centuries of artists and thinkers, statesmen and writers, men of the pen and men of the sword—women, too—have come together to populate the city. They *live* here, in the volumes of Little Journeys to the Homes of the Great, for your eternal pleasure and profit.

And this guide-book simply directs you to them by the shortest route. Many readers will appreciate the services of such a guide. It saves time. It means that your impressions will be deeper and more lasting, because more orderly.

If you will be directed by this book on your Little Journeys to the Homes of the Great, your itinerary will be sevenfold: First, the merchants, bankers, shipbuilders, and founders of industrial empires, are visited in BUSINESS AND ECONOMICS. Second, the kings and queens, generals and statesmen and revolutionists are reached in HISTORY AND GOVERNMENT. Third, you will spend some delightful days in the homes of eminent writers, orators and men of imagination in LITERATURE, ORATORY AND ROMANCE. Fourth, men of science and ingenious men who invent things will claim your rapt attention in SCIENCE AND INVENTION. Fifth, you will turn toward the highest expressions of human genius in PAINTING AND SCULPTURE. Sixth, you will advance to an appreciation of MUSIC AND POETRY as revealed by their most inspired creators. Seventh, there is inspiration and refreshment for your spirit in the cloistered walks of PHILOSOPHY AND RELIGION.

Each of the 170 "lives" which make up Little Journeys is outlined in one page of this guide-book and grouped according as it falls into one or another of the seven general branches of human knowledge. By consulting the guide-book you can have history when you wish, or business, or science, or music—whatever fits your mood or your need.

Furthermore, each of these guide-book pages supplements the inspiring biography to which it refers, with exact data—names, places, dates and facts, in compressed Baedeker style. At the same time, along with this thumb-nail encyclopaedia, you have, in Hubbard's own words, a paragraph that gives the pith and meaning of each great character—the outstanding quality that led to his greatness.

So this guide-book will be found a short-cut to intimacy with the world's outstanding geniuses. In a striking way it reveals the comprehensiveness of Hubbard's culture, and the profit you will derive from reading his Little Journeys. They provide the essentials of a liberal education in every one of the seven vital branches of human knowledge, even while they entertain, inspire and uplift!

THE EDITORS

BOOK ONE

❖

BUSINESS AND ECONOMICS

BENJAMIN FRANKLIN
JEAN JACQUES ROUSSEAU
JOSIAH WEDGWOOD
JOHN HANCOCK
MAYER ANSELM ROTHSCHILD
STEPHEN GIRARD
ALEXANDER HAMILTON
JOHN JACOB ASTOR
ROBERT OWEN
PETER COOPER
GEORGE PEABODY
WILLIAM H. SEWARD
A. T. STEWART
RICHARD COBDEN
JOHN STUART MILL
JOHN BRIGHT
PHILIP D. ARMOUR
WILLIAM MORRIS
ANDREW CARNEGIE
JAMES J. HILL
HENRY GEORGE
H. H. ROGERS
BOOKER T. WASHINGTON

BOOK TWO

❖

HISTORY AND GOVERNMENT

PERICLES
MARK ANTONY
KING ALFRED
OLIVER CROMWELL
SAMUEL ADAMS
EDMUND BURKE
GEORGE WASHINGTON
THOMAS PAINE
THOMAS JEFFERSON
JEAN PAUL MARAT
JOHN JAY
WILLIAM GODWIN
LORD NELSON
WILLIAM PITT
EMPRESS JOSEPHINE
MADAME DE STAËL
JOHN QUINCY ADAMS
HENRY CLAY
ELIZABETH FRY
DANIEL WEBSTER
THOMAS B. MACAULAY
BENJAMIN DISRAELI
GARIBALDI
ABRAHAM LINCOLN
WILLIAM E. GLADSTONE
CHARLES STEWART PARNELL

BOOK THREE

❖

LITERATURE, ORATORY, ROMANCE

DANTE ALIGHIERI
PETRARCH
WILLIAM SHAKESPEARE
FÉNELON
JONATHAN SWIFT
JOSEPH ADDISON
SAMUEL JOHNSON
PATRICK HENRY
MARY LAMB
JANE AUSTEN
THOMAS CARLYLE
MARY W. SHELLEY
HONORÉ DE BALZAC
HARRIET MARTINEAU
VICTOR HUGO
WILLIAM M. THACKERAY
WENDELL PHILLIPS
CHARLES DICKENS
HENRY WARD BEECHER
CHARLOTTE BRONTË
GEORGE ELIOT
JOHN RUSKIN
STARR KING
FERDINAND LASSALLE
DANTE GABRIEL ROSSETTI
CHARLES BRADLAUGH
ROBERT INGERSOLL
ROBERT LOUIS STEVENSON

BOOK FOUR

❖

SCIENCE AND INVENTION

LEONARDO
COPERNICUS
GALILEO
SIR ISAAC NEWTON
LINNÆUS
WILLIAM HERSCHEL
HUMBOLDT
CHARLES DARWIN
JOHN TYNDALL
JAMES OLIVER
ALFRED R. WALLACE
THOMAS H. HUXLEY
HAECKEL
JOHN FISKE
THOMAS A. EDISON

BOOK FIVE

❖

PAINTING AND SCULPTURE

BELLINI
BOTTICELLI
MICHELANGELO
TITIAN
RAPHAEL
CORREGGIO
CELLINI
RUBENS
ANTHONY VAN DYCK
VELASQUEZ
REMBRANDT
JOSHUA REYNOLDS
GAINSBOROUGH
THORWALDSEN
J. M. W. TURNER
ARY SCHEFFER
COROT
LANDSEER
FRANÇOIS MILLET
MEISSONIER
ROSA BONHEUR
GUSTAVE DORÉ
WHISTLER
FORTUNY
ABBEY

BOOK SIX

❖

MUSIC AND POETRY

JOHN MILTON
SEBASTIAN BACH
GEORGE HANDEL
OLIVER GOLDSMITH
WOLFGANG MOZART
ROBERT BURNS
LUDWIG VAN BEETHOVEN
WILLIAM WORDSWORTH
SAMUEL T. COLERIDGE
ROBERT SOUTHEY
PAGANINI
LORD BYRON
ELIZABETH B. BROWNING
FELIX MENDELSSOHN
FREDERIC CHOPIN
ALFRED TENNYSON
ROBERT SCHUMANN
FRANZ LISZT
ROBERT BROWNING
RICHARD WAGNER
GIUSEPPE VERDI
WALT WHITMAN
CHRISTINA ROSSETTI
JOHANNES BRAHMS

BOOK SEVEN

❖

PHILOSOPHY AND RELIGION

MOSES
PYTHAGORAS
CONFUCIUS
SOCRATES
PLATO
ARISTOTLE
SENECA
MARCUS AURELIUS
HYPATIA
SAINT BENEDICT
SAVONAROLA
ERASMUS
MARTIN LUTHER
JOHN KNOX
ANNE HUTCHINSON
SPINOZA
MADAME GUYON
SWEDENBORG
VOLTAIRE
JOHN WESLEY
IMMANUEL KANT
FRIEDRICH FROEBEL
SCHOPENHAUER
THOMAS ARNOLD
AUGUSTE COMTE
THEODORE PARKER
HENRY D. THOREAU
HERBERT SPENCER
MARY BAKER EDDY

BOOK ONE

❖

BUSINESS AND ECONOMICS

BENJAMIN FRANKLIN

Born 1706—Died 1790 Volume III—Page 33

FOREMOST ALL-ROUND AMERICAN

❖

"*We know of no man who ever lived a fuller life, a happier life, a life more useful to other men, than Benjamin Franklin. He gave the constant efforts of his life to his country.*"—Hubbard.

BENJAMIN FRANKLIN, whom Hubbard calls "the foremost American in point of all-round development," was born in Boston, Mass. He was intended for the ministry, but either through lack of means or an early distaste for theology perceived in the boy, the idea was abandoned in favor of an apprenticeship in an elder brother's printing shop. Benjamin seems to have mastered the trade in short order, read diligently and became a regular anonymous contributor to his brother's paper, *The New England Courant*. The brothers were not congenial, however, and young Franklin broke his indentures and slipped away by sea to New York en route to Philadelphia, where he arrived friendless and almost penniless. Within six years he was in control of the *Pennsylvania Gazette*, now the *Saturday Evening Post*. From then on he was engaged almost constantly in some sort of public activity, as editor, author, economist, scientist and statesman. He founded many public institutions that yet are flourishing. *Poor Richard's Almanac* he first published in 1732, and for twenty-five years his witty, worldly-wise sayings in it were influential in shaping the new American character. In 1753 Franklin was appointed Postmaster-General for the Colonies, and later served them on several missions abroad. He was a signer of the Declaration of Independence.

❖ ❖ ❖

What most impressed Hubbard in the life of Benjamin Franklin was his success as an all-round man. Hubbard, who retired from business with a small fortune at thirty-six, seems to have shaped his career along the lines followed by Franklin, who retired from active business at forty-two. Both men succeeded in practically everything they undertook—and the writings of both form "a model which may be studied by every one with pleasure and profit."

JEAN JACQUES ROUSSEAU

Born 1712—Died 1778 Volume IX—Page 369

FOREFATHER OF THE FRENCH REVOLUTION

❖

"*To trust humanity, he thought, was the only way humanity could be redeemed. He was the first man to say, 'That country is governed best which is governed least.'*"—Hubbard.

JEAN JACQUES ROUSSEAU, who is classified as an economist because of the great economic influence exercised by his writings, especially his *Social Contract*, which directly inspired the French Revolution and was indirectly responsible for the American War for Independence, was born at Geneva, Switzerland, and died in a suburb of Paris. He was the son of a Huguenot dancing master, who had emigrated to Switzerland in order to escape religious persecution in France. Family troubles interfered with his early education and, as recorded in his *Confessions*, Rousseau lived most of his life as a servant or tutor in successive households. The humiliating treatment to which he was subjected in the family of the French Minister at Venice, one Count de Montaign, first led him to think of the system of social distinctions then in existence, and to inquire whether any philosophical justification for them existed. Rousseau confesses to being the father of five children, all of whom he placed immediately after birth in the Home for Foundlings. His definite break with society occurred in his late forties, when he wrote his *Novel of Héloise* (1760), his *Social Contract* (1762) and his treatise on education, *Émile* (1762). These three works, so different from each other, coming from the same pen in such quick succession, established Rousseau as a thinker of his time, only to be compared with his great contemporary, Voltaire. While sojourning in England (1766-67), Rousseau wrote the greater part of his immortal *Confessions*, which were not published until after his death.

❖ ❖ ❖

From the Little Journey to Rousseau we learn that every system of business or of government (which is simply business on a major scale), is capable of improvement. Everything is going forward or backward—nothing stands still.

Josiah Wedgwood

Born 1730—Died 1795 Volume XIII—Page 49

Builder of the First Model Factory Town

❖

"*Wedgwood knew every part of his business. He modeled, made designs, mixed clay, built kilns, and at times sat up all night and fed fuel into a refractory furnace. Nothing was quite good enough—it must be better.*"—Hubbard.

JOSIAH WEDGWOOD, the famous manufacturer of pottery, who set the first example for the building of a model factory town, was born at Burslem, Staffordshire, England, and died in the town of his creation, Etruria. He was the thirteenth son of a Staffordshire potter, whose death forced the nine-year-old lad, although a confirmed cripple, to go to work as an apprentice to an elder brother. Later he associated himself with Thomas Whieldon, a prominent potter of Fenton, and in 1759 he started works of his own at Burslem, himself supplying the models and mixing the clay for his workmen. Wedgwood's interest turned especially to Etruscan vases, from which he copied his designs. In partnership with Thomas Bentley, of Liverpool, he opened, in 1769, the very extensive Etruria potteries, of which he became sole proprietor on the death of his partner. An even more important, and surviving, partner in the business was Sarah Wedgwood, a cousin, whom Josiah married after a ten-year courtship. The Wedgwood improvements in pottery, including form, substance and decoration, in all of which were attained an excellence rarely equaled, created the great trade of the Etruria potteries. He made 50 copies of the famous glass Barberini or Portland vase, which were sold for 50 guineas each, a sum which it is said did not cover the cost of production. Josiah Wedgwood published valuable pamphlets on pottery, was elected a Fellow of the Royal Society in 1783, and of the Society of Antiquaries in 1786.

❖ ❖ ❖

Hubbard was especially attracted to Josiah Wedgwood as the founder of a model community of workers along the lines of which he established his own Roycroft Shops at East Aurora. Wedgwood, being a potter, was never satisfied with making anything less than the best pottery in the world. The lesson conveyed in the Little Journey is to know your business from the ground up. Never let it outgrow you, but grow with it.

JOHN HANCOCK

Born 1737—Died 1793 Volume III—Page 99

COLONIAL PATRIOT AND MERCHANT-PRINCE

❖

"The second Congress was a Congress of action; the first had been one merely of conference. A presiding officer was required, and Samuel Adams quietly pushed his man to the front. He let it be known that Hancock was the richest man in New England, perhaps in America, and a power in every emergency."—Hubbard.

JOHN HANCOCK was born at Braintree, Mass. He graduated from Harvard in 1754, and was adopted by a wealthy uncle, on whose death in 1764 he succeeded to a fortune of £80,000, and a large mercantile business. It was the seizure of his sloop *Liberty* that occasioned a riot in 1768, when the British custom officers at Boston were mobbed. After the so-called Boston massacre two years later, Hancock was a member of the committee to demand of the British Governor Hutchinson the removal of the troops from the city, and at the funeral of the slain Americans he delivered an address so offensive to the governor that he endeavored unsuccessfully to make prisoners of Hancock and Samuel Adams. Their arrest was one of the objects of the British expedition to Concord, which resulted in the Battle of Lexington, after which General Gage offered pardon to all rebels except these two, "whose offenses are of too flagitious a nature to admit of any other consideration but that of condign punishment." In 1775, Hancock was chosen president of the Continental Congress; in 1776 signed the Declaration of Independence, and was elected first Governor of Massachusetts in 1780.

❖ ❖ ❖

John Hancock represents the big business man who also makes a success of politics and a mark in public life. Hancock inherited great wealth, but became a Boston merchant-prince on his own account. That he should have been the first signer of the Declaration of Independence, besides being the richest man in New England, furnishes an early outstanding example of hundred per cent. Americanism.

MAYER ANSELM ROTHSCHILD

Born 1743—Died 1812 Volume XI—Page 127

A GREAT BANKER

❖

"In business he was ever ready to back his opinion. He would pay 500 thalers for a jewel and pocket it silently, while the hagglers were screwing up their courage to offer 100. But—he knew what he was going to do with the jewel. He had a customer in mind. He knew the customer, he knew the jewel, and he knew his own mind."—Hubbard.

MAYER ANSELM ROTHSCHILD, founder of the family of European bankers of that name, was the son of a Jewish merchant of Frankfort, Germany. As a young man he engaged successfully in the banking business. He attracted the favorable notice of the Landgrave (afterwards Elector) of Hesse-Cassel, who, on fleeing before the French in 1806, intrusted Rothschild with the care of his private fortune derived largely from the rental of German troops to the British Government for use in quelling the American Revolution. Mayer Anselm capitalized the trust imposed in him and accumulated a large fortune. Dying, he left five sons, all of whom were made Barons by the Emperor of Austria in 1822. The oldest, Mayer Anselm, carried on the business at Frankfort, where he died without issue. Solomon became head of a banking house at Vienna, while Nathan, perhaps the ablest of the sons, conducted the London house. It was Nathan who greatly enhanced the family fortunes by speculating upon the defeat of Napoleon at Waterloo. At the end of the first stage of the battle, of which he was a witness, he shrewdly foresaw a victory for the allies under the Duke of Wellington, and turned it to his advantage on the London Stock Exchange.

❖ ❖ ❖

Never was there a better illustration of the value of a reputation for trustworthiness than is afforded by Mayer A. Rothschild. The Landgrave of Hesse-Cassel placed in his keeping some $2,000,000 without asking for a receipt. Hubbard shows here that trustworthiness is fully as important as shrewdness and ability in the achievement of business success.

STEPHEN GIRARD

Born 1750—Died 1831 Volume XI—Page 93

A FEARLESS MERCHANT

❖

"When near the close of the War of 1812 the Government was trying to float a loan of five million dollars, Girard stepped forward and took the entire loan, although it was really more than his entire fortune. The effect was magical. If Old Girard was not afraid, the people were not. He believed in America and in her future."—Hubbard.

STEPHEN GIRARD, whom Hubbard couples with Benjamin Franklin in the list of citizens extraordinary of Philadelphia, was born at Bordeaux, France, the son of a sea captain. At the age of thirteen he ran away from home, became a sailor, and six years later was captain and part owner of a ship engaged in the West Indian and American coasting trade. In 1769 he settled in Philadelphia, but continued in the coasting trade until stopped by the outbreak of the Revolutionary War. Espousing the cause of the Colonies, he remained in America, dealt in a small way in army supplies, and in 1780 re-embarked in the West Indian trade, meeting with such success in a series of lucky ventures that he accumulated a considerable fortune. At the time of his death Girard left an estate of about $7,500,000, the largest in America up to that time. Girard invested largely in shares of the old Bank of the United States in 1810, and in 1812 upon the lapsing of its charter, he purchased a controlling interest and the building in which the business was conducted. He named it the Bank of Stephen Girard and made it the foremost banking house in the country. During the War of 1812 Girard was the financial mainstay of the United States Government; in 1814 he subscribed for about 95 per cent. of the war loan of $5,000,000. For the erection and maintenance of Girard College, a school for white orphans, in Philadelphia, he left about $5,260,000.

❖ ❖ ❖

As recorded in this Little Journey, Stephen Girard put fear out of his life forever. Other eminent merchants have been courageous in their business ventures, but Girard was as fearless of death as he was of anything in life. Said he, "Fear is the only devil!"

ALEXANDER HAMILTON

Born 1757—Died 1804 Volume III—Page 153

FIRST AMERICAN BUSINESS STATESMAN

❖

"*Hamilton was evolving that financial policy, broad, comprehensive and minute, which endures even to this day. . . . His insistence that to preserve the credit of a nation every debt must be paid, is an idea that no statesman now dare question.*"—Hubbard.

ALEXANDER HAMILTON was born at Charles Town, on the island of Nevis, West Indies, and died in New York City from a bullet wound received in a duel with Aaron Burr. His mother was of Huguenot descent, the daughter of a French physician, unhappily married to John Michel Lavine, a Danish land proprietor of Saint Croix, whom she left to live with a Scotch planter named Hamilton, to whom she bore Alexander and another son. His father failed in business when the future American statesman-financier-economist was 12 years old, and he had to earn his own living. His "genius for affairs" was soon apparent, and at the age of 15 he was sent to America to be educated. He secured a captaincy in the Continental Army, 1776, participated in the Battles of Long Island, White Plains, Trenton and Princeton, and won the commendation of his superiors. Later he was an aide-de-camp and private secretary to Washington, who entrusted him with the important and delicate mission of going to Albany to obtain troops from the recalcitrant General Gates. While on this mission he met Elizabeth, daughter of General Philip Schuyler, whom he married in 1780. On the creation of a Treasury Department in 1789, Hamilton became its first Secretary, reduced the confused finances to order, provided for a funded system and a sound system of taxation, induced Congress to assume the State debts, authorized methods for the establishing of a national bank and mint and an internal revenue service. Hamilton resigned from the Washington Cabinet in 1795.

❖ ❖ ❖

Alexander Hamilton's success in bringing order out of chaos in the finances of the young Republic was due mainly to his confidence and belief in himself. Those qualities were so pronounced as to be shared by everyone who knew him, and put him in line for constant advancement.

JOHN JACOB ASTOR

Born 1763—Died 1848 Volume XI—Page 203

AMERICA'S FIRST GREAT LANDLORD

❖

"*Astor hated gamblers. He never confused gambling, as a mode of money-getting, with actual production. He knew that gambling produces nothing—it merely transfers wealth, changes ownership. And since it involves loss of time and energy it is a positive waste.*"—Hubbard.

THE original John Jacob Astor, a pioneer American merchant, was born in Waldorf, a village near Heidelburg, Germany. His father was a butcher. At the age of twenty John Jacob Astor followed an elder brother, first to London and then to New York, where he engaged in the fur trade, dealing directly with the Indians. At first he prepared the furs with his own hands and took them to the London market. Despite the growing influence of the English fur-trading companies in North America, he fitted out two expeditions to the Oregon Territory—one by land and one by sea—for the purpose of opening up regular commercial intercourse with the natives. After many mishaps, his object was achieved in 1811 and the fur-trading station of Astoria was established, but the War of 1812 ended its prosperity. Astor lost in the neighborhood of a million dollars by the venture. Subsequently engaging in the China trade, he was eminently successful. His commercial connections extended over the entire globe and his ships were familiar to every sea. In 1827 he and his son, William, who had been his partner since 1815, withdrew from the China trade and formed the American Fur Company. A few years later the elder Astor retired from business altogether, devoting himself to his investments. His estate at the time of his death, in 1848, amounted to $30,000,000, largely invested in real estate on Manhattan Island.

❖ ❖ ❖

John Jacob Astor possessed one preëminent quality that made him a multimillionaire. It was foresight. When New York City had less than 100,000 population, he foresaw its phenomenal growth and bought real estate that enhanced enormously in value. In the Little Journey it is made clear that the opportunity given Astor to so invest his money was open to everybody, but he alone took advantage of it to the limit of his resources.

ROBERT OWEN

Born 1771—Died 1858 Volume XI—Page 11

FIRST MODERN BUSINESSMAN

❖

"Robert Owen wanted nothing for himself which the world could not have on the same terms. . . . His desire was to benefit mankind, and to help himself by helping others."—Hubbard.

ROBERT OWEN, whom Hubbard calls "the world's first businessman," in the modern meaning of the term, was born at Newton, Montgomeryshire, North Wales. His parents were poor, and at the age of ten he was apprenticed to a draper. He developed remarkable powers of organization and at 18 became superintendent of a Manchester, England, cotton mill employing 500 hands. In 1799 he married the daughter of one David Dale, proprietor of extensive cotton-mills at New Lanark, Scotland, of which he became director and part-owner the following year. He achieved a wide reputation, both for its industrial success and the prosperity of the workmen. Owen provided recreation centers for them, stopped the employment of young children and inaugurated a system of education far in advance of his time. In 1813 the business was reorganized, giving Owen a freer hand for his philanthropic schemes and yielding a good interest on the investment. New Lanark became famous and attracted distinguished visitors from all parts of the world. In 1824, Owen came to America and founded a community at New Harmony, Indiana, across the Ohio from what is now Owensboro, Kentucky. Throughout his later life he labored tirelessly to better social conditions in manufacturing centers.

❖ ❖ ❖

That the square deal pays in business is emphasized throughout the Little Journey to Robert Owen, a pioneer in practising, as well as preaching, the precept that both sides should profit in every business transaction. Owen is the first businessman on record to regard private business as a public trust. His is a striking example of the way to achieve success through winning and capitalizing confidence.

PETER COOPER

Born 1791—Died 1883 Volume XI—Page 233

PIONEER AMERICAN CAPTAIN OF INDUSTRY

❖

"*Peter Cooper craved the excitement of adventure. His nature demanded new schemes, new plans, new methods. . . . A glue factory was the foundation of his fortune. He never referred to it as a chemical laboratory, nor did he call it a studio. He was proud of his business.*" —Hubbard.

PETER COOPER, designated by Hubbard as "America's first businessman," was born and died in New York City. Notable by turns as an inventor, manufacturer and philanthropist, he began his career as apprentice to a coach-maker. He invented a machine for sheering cloth, which was used extensively during the War of 1812, when material for military uniforms was scarce. For a time he conducted a corner-grocery business, and finally established a glue and isinglass factory, continuing the business for more than fifty years and acquiring great wealth. In 1828 he built large iron-works in Baltimore, and afterwards a rolling and wire mill in the neighborhood of New York and blast furnaces in Pennsylvania. Two years later he designed and built the first American locomotive engine to be operated successfully, a rude contrivance, which he exhibited on what came to be the Baltimore and Ohio Railroad; and about 1845 he made at Trenton, New Jersey, the first rolled-iron beams for building purposes. With Cyrus W. Field he was a pioneer in promoting the laying of the Atlantic cable, and for many years was president of the New York, Newfoundland and London Telegraph Company. In 1876 Peter Cooper received the Independent nomination for President of the United States. In gratitude for his success in many forms of mercantile life, and wishing to afford others opportunities which he himself had never enjoyed, he established in 1854 what is known as Cooper Union, in New York City, by which he is best remembered.

❖ ❖ ❖

Peter Cooper maintained an open mind to the end of his long, useful life, and was never afraid to attempt new enterprises. Versatility is not usually regarded as a business asset, but Cooper was an exception that proves the rule. He engaged in many lines of business and was successful in all.

GEORGE PEABODY

Born 1795—Died 1869 Volume XI—Page 303

WORLD'S FIRST PHILANTHROPIST

❖

"In childhood, poverty was the portion of George Peabody. . . . But he succeeded, for he had the persistent corpuscle, and he had charm of manner—two things which will make any man a winner in the game of life. . . ."—Hubbard.

GEORGE PEABODY, whom Hubbard entitles "the world's first philanthropist," was born at Danvers (now Peabody), Massachusetts, and was buried there after dying in London, England, the home of his later years. Dependent upon himself for support, he went at the age of sixteen or seventeen to Washington, D. C., and engaged in the dry goods business, at first as a pedler. He saw service as a volunteer in the War of 1812, and later became associated with Elisha Riggs in business. The firm moved to Baltimore, Maryland, in 1815, and prospered. Twenty years later, when the State of Maryland was threatened with bankruptcy, Peabody headed a commission which negotiated an $8,000,000 loan in London, and saved the credit of the State. Later (retaining a branch office in Baltimore) he founded the house of George Peabody & Company in London, and remained there until his death. During his long absence from the United States he never lost interest in American affairs, as shown by his successive benefactions. He contributed liberally to promote the American exhibit at the first World's Fair of 1851, in London; helped finance the Kane expedition of 1851 in search of Sir John Franklin in the arctic regions; founded and endowed the Peabody Institute at Baltimore; gave $3,000,000 to promote education in the Southern States and a similar sum to build lodging houses for the poor of London, among other philanthropies. Such munificence, then without parallel, brought him gratitude and honor from England and the United States. Queen Victoria offered him a baronetcy, which he declined, preferring a letter from the queen, which he received and placed in the library which bears his name in his native Massachusetts town.

❖ ❖ ❖

Charm of manner, which George Peabody preëminently possessed, was his chief stock in trade, and smoothed the way for his great career as merchant, banker and philanthropist. In the Little Journey to the Home of Peabody it is shown that this beneficent human quality called charm is based upon glowing physical health, absolute honesty and good-will.

WILLIAM H. SEWARD

Born 1801—Died 1872 Volume III—Page 255

GREAT CIVIL WAR STATESMAN-ECONOMIST

❖

"*Seward was a man of positive ideas. . . . His clear insight into practical things, backed by the quiet working energy of his nature, brought about many changes, and the changes he effected and the reforms he inaugurated must ever rank his name high among statesmen. . . . Largely through his efforts, a safe and general banking system was brought about.*"—Hubbard.

WILLIAM HENRY SEWARD, statesman-economist, whose fame rests largely upon the work he accomplished as Secretary of State in the Lincoln Cabinet, was a native of Florida, Orange County, N. Y. At twenty-one he was admitted to the bar, and in 1823 located at Auburn, N. Y., to practice law. In 1830 he was elected to the State Senate by the Anti-Masonic Party, to whose first national convention he was a delegate. As a legislator he won distinction by his industry and ability in advocating internal improvements, support of the common schools, and reforms of various kinds. As agent of the Holland Land Company, he laid the foundation of a private fortune. In 1838 Seward was elected Governor of New York. His term was marked by anti-rent troubles growing out of a revolt of tenants in a number of New York counties against feudal landlordism. Lawlessness became prevalent, and murders frequent. Going to the United States Senate in 1849, Seward was thereafter a national figure. Defeated for the Republican Presidential nomination in 1860, on the election of Abraham Lincoln he became one of the great American Secretaries of State, serving in the Lincoln Cabinet through the Civil War and after. An attempt was made on his life the day that Lincoln was assassinated, April 14, 1865. Besides negotiating many important treaties with foreign countries, Seward arranged with Russia for the purchase of Alaska for $7,200,000.

❖ ❖ ❖

William H. Seward is an example of the young man who gets ahead under the most discouraging circumstances. Ill-equipped physically, like Daniel Webster, he was only given an education because he was not strong enough to work. Yet, as Hubbard says, Abraham Lincoln was never wiser than when he secured Seward as Secretary of State.

A. T. STEWART

Born 1803—Died 1876 Volume XI—Page 335

AMERICA'S FIRST GREAT RETAIL MERCHANT

❖

"We can truthfully say that there is not a successful retail store in America that does not show the influence of A. T. Stewart. . . . He was a natural salesman . . . who seems to have been the very first man in trade to realize that to hold your trade you must make a friend of the customer. He was alive, alert and sensitive to the spirit of the times." —Hubbard.

ALEXANDER TURNEY STEWART, the foremost American department store merchant of the middle nineteenth century, and, as Hubbard records, originator of the "One-Price" system, was born at Lisburn, near Belfast, Ireland. For a time he attended Trinity College at Dublin, but before graduating he emigrated to the United States in 1823 and at first taught school in New York City. In 1825, having fallen heir to a small legacy, he embarked in the retail drygoods business and was so successful that in 1848 he occupied a store built for him by John Jacob Astor at Broadway and Chambers Street, New York, that for many years remained the largest retail establishment in the world. In 1862 he removed his retail business to a new store, which he erected at a cost of $2,750,000 on Broadway, between Ninth and Tenth Streets, retaining his old store for wholesale trade. At the time of his death the business of A. T. Stewart & Company comprised branches and agencies in the principal cities of Europe, and several mills and factories in the United States. His body was interred in Saint Mark's church-yard, New York, from which the ashes were stolen in 1878. They were afterward recovered and deposited in the mausoleum of the Cathedral of the Incarnation, erected by his widow in memory of her husband at Garden City, Long Island.

❖ ❖ ❖

A. T. Stewart launched the One-Price idea in American business and built a fortune on the business principle of making a lasting friend of every customer. His great success was due primarily to his original methods of doing business. He was constantly breaking new ground, such as inaugurating the "money back if not satisfied" policy, the Cost Sale, the Fire Sale.

RICHARD COBDEN

Born 1804—Died 1865 Volume IX—Page 127

FATHER OF FREE TRADE

❖

"Cobden, who had never had any chance in life, at thirty, with an income equal to thirty-five thousand dollars a year, was at the head of a constantly growing business. He had acquired the study habit ten years before, so really we need shed no tears on account of his lack of college training."—Hubbard.

RICHARD COBDEN, the English manufacturer, statesman and economist known as the Father of Free Trade, was a native of Sussex, England. Employed at the age of 14 by an uncle, who had a warehouse in London, he became a commercial traveler at 21, and seven years later branched out as the agent of a large manufacturing house in Manchester on a capital consisting mainly of energy, ability and his good name. By 1831 he had prospered sufficiently to become a textile manufacturer at Sabden, England. The "Cobden prints" became famous, and their originator was on the way to the accumulation of a large fortune. However, he practically retired from business, and spent the years from 1832 to 1835 acquiring the knowledge of political history and economics for which he was distinguished. He became convinced that commerce was the great torch-bearer of civilization and the foundation of all national prosperity. Anything, therefore, which interfered with the free exchange of commodities between nations was harmful, and for this reason protection, which damned the current of trade, and war, which sought entirely to destroy it, were pernicious. Out of his convictions grew the Anti-Corn-Law League, organized in 1839, of which Cobden and six others constituted the council. In 1841 he entered Parliament, and within five years had converted Sir Robert Peel, the English Prime Minister, and his party to free trade. During the Corn Laws agitation Cobden neglected his business entirely and became impoverished. A popular subscription of £80,000 or more was raised to enable him to remain in Parliament.

❖ ❖ ❖

Hubbard found in Richard Cobden a business executive to pattern after. Cobden never did anything himself that he could employ someone else to do for him. In other words, he left the details to others and reserved his great ability for the work which no one else could do so well.

JOHN STUART MILL

Born 1806—Died 1873 Volume XIII—Page 143

FOREMOST THINKER OF HIS TIME

❖

"When Mill was thirty . . . practical business had sobered him. The modesty, gentleness and dignity of the man made his presence felt wherever he went. . . . His whole aspect was one of high and noble achievement—invincible purpose, iron will, unflinching self-oblivion."—Hubbard.

JOHN STUART MILL, son of James Mill, a British economist and philosopher of only lesser distinction, was born in London and died at Avignon, France. He was educated at home by his father who began teaching him Greek at three and never permitted him to indulge in childhood recreations. At the age of seventeen he entered the India House as a clerk under his father, who was assistant (later chief) examiner of the department in control of Indian administration—political, judicial and financial. For thirty-three years John Stuart Mill was in the service of this company, gradually rising till at last he was head of his department. When the government of India was transferred to the Crown in 1858, he retired from office on an adequate pension. In 1865 Mill was elected to Parliament, aligned himself with the advanced Radicals, and urged the extension of suffrage to women. In 1851 he married Harriet Taylor, widow of a wealthy London stock broker, during whose lifetime Mrs. Taylor and Mill had maintained quite unconventional relations. She died in 1859. At twenty-nine Mill became editor of the *London and Westminster Review*, in which his first writings appeared. He edited this important journal over a period of six years. His chief works are *A System of Logic*, *Principles of Political Economy*, *On Liberty*, *The Subjection of Women* and his *Autobiography*.

❖ ❖ ❖

Mill formulated the doctrine of the greatest good to the greatest number, which Henry Ford has applied in urging that the best policy for employers to pursue is to pay the highest instead of the lowest possible wages. Mill himself was a thinker who made thinking pay. To be a success as an idealist it is not necessary to be a failure in practical affairs, is the lesson conveyed in the Little Journey to John Stuart Mill.

JOHN BRIGHT

Born 1811—Died 1889 Volume IX—Page 217

A GREAT BUSINESSMAN IN POLITICS

❖

"*Not only did he carry on a great private business, and at the same time bear heavy burdens in the management of his country's affairs, but he was always a student, always a learner, and also always a teacher. . . .*" —Hubbard.

JOHN BRIGHT was the son of a Quaker cotton-spinner and manufacturer, whose business he inherited and conducted with eminent success in Lancashire, England. His education was meager, and the splendid attainments of his later life must be ascribed entirely to his own ability and industry. He entered the business at 15, and even at that early age showed marked sagacity and energy. Not satisfied, however, with merely mercantile affairs, he took an enthusiastic interest in the abolition of slavery and other public questions of the day. In 1839 he associated himself with Richard Cobden in organizing the famous Anti-Corn-Law League, and subsequently threw himself passionately into the movement, until the Corn Laws were repealed in 1846. Bright was elected to Parliament in 1843 and served several terms in the House of Commons, coming to be regarded as a leader of English workingmen. He gave much attention to the Irish question, advocating the disestablishment of the Irish Church, and to the end of his life was interested in the various Irish land-measures. He held a Cabinet office under Gladstone. In 1883 he was made Lord Rector of Glasgow University. The enormous influence which Bright exercised on English politics and public opinion during the greater part of his life was due to his high moral character as well as mentality. Though called the Tribune of the People, he never feared to antagonize public opinion whenever it did not conform to his rigid standards of duty and right.

❖ ❖ ❖

Bright was rich enough to be free from temptation and to act according to his convictions, even against his own immediate interests. His support of the Union cause in our Civil War, which threatened his cotton-spinning business with ruin, is an instance.

PHILIP D. ARMOUR

Born 1832—Died 1901 Volume XI—Page 167

FOUNDER OF THE PACKING INDUSTRY

❖

"*Philip D. Armour was a man of big mental and physical resources—big in brain, rich in vital power, bold in initiative, yet cautious.*"—Hubbard.

PHILIP DANFORTH ARMOUR, American merchant and philanthropist, was a native of Stockbridge, New York. At the age of nineteen he made the arduous overland journey to California, in the wake of the "gold rush," but returned east four years later and established himself in the commission business in Milwaukee, Wisconsin, becoming a partner of John Plankington. In 1870 he transferred the business to Chicago and organized the pork and beef packing firm of Armour and Company. The business increased with great rapidity and its products were exported to every land. Armour also engaged in —virtually originated—the refrigerator car service, and at the time of his death controlled more grain elevators than any other man or group of men in the world. On his payroll were more than 50,000 employees. He endowed the Armour Institute of Technology and the Armour Mission, both in Chicago, the combined endowments of which aggregated $2,500,000. The purpose of the Institute has been "to give young men an opportunity to secure a liberal technical education." Its founder, "realizing the importance of self-reliance as a factor in the development of character, has conditioned his benefactions in such a way as to emphasize both their value and the student's self-respect."

❖ ❖ ❖

Philip D. Armour not only originated the modern packing house, but he, more than anyone else, developed it into the second or third largest industry in the country. What Hubbard brings out in this Little Journey is the importance of keeping abreast of scientific progress in business and utilizing, as Armour did, every agency that can promote growth in the performance of industrial service.

WILLIAM MORRIS

Born 1834—Died 1896 Volume V—Page 11

MASTER OF MANY CRAFTS

❖

"To the influence of William Morris does the civilized world owe its salvation from the mad rage and rush for the tawdry and cheap in home decoration. . . . He was the strongest all-round man the century has produced. . . ."—Hubbard.

WILLIAM MORRIS, whom Hubbard describes as a great artist, economist and master of six distinct trades, was born near London, England, his father being a prosperous stock broker. He attended Exeter College, Oxford, where he formed an important and lasting friendship with Edward Burne-Jones, the artist, with whom he was afterwards associated in his celebrated artcrafts enterprises. It was in 1861 that Morris, in association with Burne-Jones, Dante Gabriel Rossetti and other friends, established a firm in London for designing and manufacturing artistic furniture and household decorations. Subsequently was added the manufacture of tapestry and other textiles, dyeing, book-illumination and printing. The original firm was dissolved in 1871; and in 1881 Morris transferred the works to Merton in Surrey, England. Nine years later was founded the famous Kelmscott Press at Hammersmith on the upper Thames. For the practical advancement of the arts and crafts, and of the doctrine that all things should be made beautiful, Morris did more than any other man of his time. He also was a distinguished romantic poet and author. In later life he became an active Socialist and a leader of the Socialistic League in England. Morris died leaving to the world an immortal example of the man who devotes his wealth and his genius to the bettering of living conditions and to the spread of ideals.

❖ ❖ ❖

William Morris gave Hubbard the idea for the Roycroft Shops, which were founded on the principle that art is the expression of a man's joy in his work. Hubbard came back from his visit to Morris at the Kelmscott Press convinced that one could get as much profit and infinitely more personal satisfaction by producing a sound, high-grade article than a cheap and shoddy one. "Not how cheap, but how good," was both the Kelmscott and the Roycroft motto.

ANDREW CARNEGIE

Born 1835—Died 1919 Volume XI—Page 263

GREAT IRONMASTER AND PHILANTHROPIST

❖

"Carnegie never was a speculator. He was no gambler. He never bought a share of stock on margin in his life. The only thing he ever bet on was his ability."—Hubbard.

ANDREW CARNEGIE, whose industrial genius and Scotch shrewdness even in philanthropy are extolled by Hubbard, was a native of Dunfermline, Scotland. None of the great makers of their own fortunes began nearer to absolute zero. His success came through steady labor, sagacity and self-culture plus the faculty of capitalizing opportunities open to all and less to him than to most. His father's small hand-loom business was ruined in 1848 by the competition of steam. The family emigrated to America, settling in Pittsburgh, Pennsylvania, where 10-year-old Andrew became a bobbin-boy at 20 cents a day. Presently he was a telegraph messenger, then a telegrapher and next a train dispatcher for the Pennsylvania Railroad, whose general superintendent made Carnegie his secretary. During the Civil War Carnegie was in charge of the eastern military railroads and telegraph lines. Foreseeing the use of iron in bridges, he organized the Keystone Bridge Works which built the first iron bridge across the Ohio. His future business career was thus determined. Having consolidated all his interests in the Carnegie Steel Company in 1901, he transferred it at a valuation of $500,000,000 to be merged into the United States Steel Corporation. In philanthropy Carnegie is best remembered as the donor of the Carnegie Libraries and various Hero Funds.

❖ ❖ ❖

From Andrew Carnegie we learn the value of spare time. It was in his leisure hours that this Scotch immigrant boy acquired the reading habit, mastered telegraphy, investigated steel processes and made himself ready to grasp opportunities.

JAMES J. HILL

Born 1838—Died 1916 Volume XI—Page 401

A GREAT RAILROAD BUILDER

❖

"*As the extraordinary part of James J. Hill's career did not begin until he was forty years of age, our romantic friends who write of him often picture him as a failure up to that time. The fact is, he was making head and gathering gear right along. . . . To gain possession of the railroad and run it so as to build up the country, and thus prosper as the farmers prospered, was his ambition.*"—Hubbard.

JAMES JEROME HILL, who contributed more than any other man to the phenomenal development of the northwestern part of the United States, was born near Guelph, Ontario, Canada, and died at Saint Paul, Minn., having settled there forty years previously. As clerk or agent he was at first employed in the Mississippi River steamboat business, and in 1870 he established the Red River Transportation Company, operating between Saint Paul and Winnipeg, Manitoba. Through this enterprise he obtained an idea of the immense coming importance of transportation in the Northwest, and in 1878 he was one of a syndicate that bought the defaulted bonds of the Saint Paul and Pacific Railroad Company. On its reorganization as the Saint Paul, Minneapolis and Manitoba Railway Company he became general manager, and in 1881 and 1882 vice-president and president progressively. The latter office he held for 25 years, during which time the road was extended westward to Seattle, on Puget Sound, and eastward to Duluth, on Lake Superior. By 1890 all the lines of the system were united in the Great Northern Company which, together with the Northern Pacific, in 1901 acquired the Chicago, Burlington and Quincy Railroad Company. James J. Hill resigned as president of the combined system in 1907 to become chairman of the board of directors, being succeeded in the former office by his son, L. W. Hill.

❖ ❖ ❖

James J. Hill shows us the part that vision and imagination play in business. He foresaw the vast agricultural empire to be opened up in northwestern America through the development of railroad transportation. The value of foresight in business is increasing every year through the development of science and invention, higher standards of living and the greater demands of civilization.

HENRY GEORGE

Born 1839—Died 1897 Volume IX—Page 55

SINGLE TAX APOSTLE

❖

"*The remedy Henry George prescribed for economic ills was as simple as it was new: Let the land gravitate to the people who have the disposition and the ability to improve it—and that is just what the Single Tax will do. . . .*"—Hubbard.

HENRY GEORGE was a native of Philadelphia, designed by William Penn to be a City of Brotherly Love. Thrown upon his own resources at the age of 14, he shipped before the mast, later became a "printer's devil," and in 1858 worked his way as a sailor to California. For several years he drifted from one employment to another, including the publication of a San Francisco daily newspaper. The venture was a failure. He then became a reporter on another now defunct journal, of which he became editor-in-chief, at the same time acting as correspondent for the New York *Tribune*. To the *Tribune* he contributed, in 1869, an article on the Chinese question, which was commended by the English economist John Stuart Mill. The great fortunes acquired in California through the rapid increase in land values fixed his attention upon the land problem; and in a pamphlet published in 1871, entitled *Our Land Policy*, Henry George advanced most of the ideas that distinguish his later and most famous work, *Progress and Poverty*. The George doctrine is that the value of land represents in the main a monopoly power, and that the entire burden of taxation should be levied upon it, thus freeing industry from taxation, and equalizing opportunities by destroying monopoly advantage. This book later enjoyed a wide American circulation. In 1886 George was a candidate for the mayoralty of New York City, but was defeated by Abram S. Hewitt. In 1897 he again was a candidate, but died before election day.

❖ ❖ ❖

Henry George held that wages are not paid out of capital, but out of the value which the workers themselves create. Hubbard shared with them the belief that the man who lives on the labor of others, without producing anything himself, is worse than useless.

H. H. Rogers

Born 1840—Died 1909 Volume XI—Page 359

Ideal Captain of Industry

❖

"H. H. Rogers was the typical American, and his career was the ideal one to which we are always pointing our growing youth. He had the splendid ability to say 'No' when he should."—Hubbard.

HENRY HUDDLESTON ROGERS, whom Hubbard characterizes as "an ideal captain of industry," was born at Fairhaven, Massachusetts, when that seaport was still sharing with New Bedford and other New England seaboard towns the prosperity that attended the whaling industry. He was educated in the schools of his native town, and afterwards was identified with the Standard Oil Company, of which he was an original stockholder, eventually becoming a vice-president. He was also president of the Amalgamated Copper Company; director of the United States Steel Corporation and numerous other large enterprises. Of the great wealth acquired by him in business he devoted large sums to public and benevolent uses, especially for the benefit of his native town. Among his gifts to it are two schools, a town hall, the Millicent Library (a memorial to a deceased daughter), a Masonic building and memorial church buildings, the chief structure of a group being perhaps the finest example of Tudor architecture in America. H. H. Rogers also built at Fairhaven, and presented to the Millicent Library, a system of waterworks from which it derives an income. An enterprise on which he was engaged at the time of his death was the building of the Virginian Railroad at a cost to himself of approximately $40,000,000. It is 443 miles long, and connects the great coal-fields of West Virginia with the Atlantic seaboard.

❖ ❖ ❖

Hubbard calls the subject of this Little Journey an ideal captain of industry, because he was preëminently able, straightforward and courageous. His life constitutes the complete American business romance. Rogers was a dreamer—of dreams that he made come true.

Booker T. Washington

Born 1858—Died 1915 Volume X—Page 185

A Great Negro Uplifter

❖

"Booker T. Washington set out to help the Negro win success for himself by serving society through becoming skilled in doing useful things. . . . He collected upward of six million dollars, mostly from the people of the North, and built up the nearest perfect educational institution in the world."—Hubbard.

BOOKER TALIAFERRO WASHINGTON, the founder and for thirty-four years business director of Tuskegee Institute, was born in Franklin County, Virginia. He was a plantation slave, and as a child was taken to Malden, West Virginia, where he worked first in a salt-furnace and afterwards in a coal-mine, obtaining his first instruction in a local night school. After much difficulty and hardship he made his way to the Hampton (Va.) Normal and Agricultural Institute, where he paid his way for three years by working as janitor. In 1879 he was appointed an instructor at Hampton, and displayed such ability that, in 1881, he was selected by General S. C. Armstrong, head of the school, to start a similar institution at Tuskegee, Alabama. The State Legislature granted an annual appropriation of $2,000 to pay the instructors. Washington opened the school in a dilapidated shanty and a church, with 30 pupils, and himself the only teacher. Subsequently he transferred the school to its present site on a plantation he bought for $500, about a mile from Tuskegee. His efforts in developing the institution brought into play his remarkable powers of organization and revealed him as an economist of the first order. His aim was to give the blacks a practical education in the trades and industries, leading to an ultimate position of economic independence. The enrollment at Tuskegee is now about 2,000, and the faculty has nearly 300 members.

❖ ❖ ❖

Born a slave, the subject of this Little Journey proves how high one can climb who starts even lower than the ordinary bottom rung of the ladder. In view of what Booker Washington accomplished, nobody in this broad land of opportunity has any good excuse for being discouraged.

BOOK TWO

❖

HISTORY AND GOVERNMENT

PERICLES

Born 495 B. C.—Died 429 B. C. Volume VII—Page 11

THE GREATEST OF GREEK STATESMEN

❖

"*Pericles built and maintained a State, and he did it by recognizing and binding to him ability. It is a fine thing to have ability, but the ability to discover ability in others is the true test.*"—Hubbard.

PERICLES was the son of Xanthippus, victor over the Persians at Mycale in 479 B. C. His eloquence, sagacity, uprightness and patriotism won recognition, and for more than thirty years he was the most influential leader in Athens. Under his leadership its complete democratization was accomplished. Hitherto only the nobler and richer citizens were eligible for the higher offices, but Pericles threw down all barriers, even the Senators being chosen by lot from the entire body of Athenians. Following a series of military triumphs over the Corinthians, Spartans and Persians, Pericles concluded a peace treaty and formed the Confederacy of Delos dominated by Athens. With the great wealth accumulated during the years of conquest, Pericles restored the Athenian temples that had been destroyed by the Persians and erected new monuments which made Athens the most splendid city of ancient times. Prominent among them were the bronze statue of Athena Promachos, erected about 448 B. C. at the west end of the Acropolis, and a new temple to Athena Polias. The Parthenon was also rebuilt on a more magnificent scale. Pericles was a great military, as well as political, leader, as was shown by his reduction of Samos in 439 and in the first part of the Peloponnesian war.

❖ ❖ ❖

Pericles, who was equally great as an orator, musician, philosopher, architect, financier and practical administrator, proves the possibility of a man making a success of any kind of work he undertakes.

Mark Antony

Born 83 B. C.—Died 30 B. C. Volume VII—Page 43

A Great Roman Triumvir

❖

"In the stress of defeat and impending calamity, Mark Antony was a great man; he could endure anything but success. . . . Unlike Cæsar the Great he was no scholar, so books were not a solace; to build up and beautify a great State did not occur to him."—Hubbard.

MARK ANTONY, son of a Roman prætor, was related through his mother to Julius Cæsar, whose assassination was the subject of his famous funeral oration. Following a youth of dissipation, Antony entered the army and in the war between Cæsar and Pompey he commanded the Cæsarian legions in Italy. His valor at Pharsalia caused Cæsar to let him govern Italy during his own absence in Africa. As a Roman consul, in 47 B. C., he sought to have Cæsar recognized as emperor. Turning the murder of Cæsar to his own advantage, Antony's power was absolute for a time before he was forced to share it with young Octavius (the future Augustus) Cæsar and Lepidus. After making Italy safe for themselves, Antony and Octavius led an army against Brutus and Cassius in Macedonia and were victorious at Philippi, 42 B. C. Antony proceeded to Egypt to settle a dispute with Cleopatra, and was captivated by the Egyptian queen. Recalled to Italy, to placate Octavius, Antony married his sister, Octavia, but soon abandoned her and returned to Egypt and Cleopatra. War followed, in which the forces of Antony and Cleopatra were defeated by those of Octavius at Actium, 31 B. C. Antony and Cleopatra committed suicide.

❖ ❖ ❖

Mark Antony, whose qualities of loyalty, all-round capacity and faithful performance of duty made him what Hubbard calls "the right hand of Caesar," is a signal example of the man who is a greater follower than leader. Such a person works to best advantage under proper direction. Yet it is possible for such a man to develop powers of genuine leadership, such as Antony displayed under the spur of necessity.

KING ALFRED

Born 849—Died 901 Volume X—Page 125

FOUNDER OF THE ANGLO-SAXON RACE

❖

"The English love of law, system and order dates from Alfred. In him were combined the virtues of the scholar and patriot, the efficiency of the man of affairs with the wisdom of the philosopher. . . . His whole life was one of enlightened and magnanimous service to his country."
—Hubbard.

ALFRED, known as the Great, was born at Wantage, in Berkshire, England. He was the youngest of five sons of Æthelwulf, king of the West Saxons, and ascended the throne on the death of an elder brother in 871. His reign of more than thirty years is noteworthy because of the wars he engaged in with Danish invaders and because of the interest he took in education. Alfred became king in the midst of one of the Danish invasions that had an important influence on the history of England. By crushing the individual kingdoms, the successive invaders worked, unwittingly, for the unity of England. Alfred, by withstanding them successfully, made his kingdom the rallying point for all the Saxons, and prepared the way for the eventual supremacy of his descendants. As Hubbard records, Alfred was an enthusiastic scholar and a zealous patron of learning. Attaining the throne, as he himself wrote, he found little or no interest in education, and few learned men. He invited to his court native and foreign scholars, notably Asser and John Scotus Erigena. Alfred constantly labored himself, and encouraged others to labor, for the education of his people. He modestly disclaimed originality for the laws he compiled, but they are distinguished for their religious character and for making no distinction between English and Welsh rules of conduct and property rights, as the earlier laws had done.

❖ ❖ ❖

King Alfred ranks as one of the great teachers of mankind because he first taught the English, or rather Anglo-Saxon, people that education is necessary to civilization. In educating his subjects Alfred educated himself—became, in fact, the best educated man of his time. As Hubbard frequently observes in the Little Journeys, the best way to learn a thing oneself is to teach it to others.

OLIVER CROMWELL

Born 1599—Died 1658 Volume IX—Page 305

GREAT ENGLISH FIGHTING REFORMER

❖

"Cromwell's greatest successes were snatched from the teeth of defeat. He always had a few extra links to let out. When others were ready to quit, he had just begun. Like Paul Jones, when called upon to surrender he shouted back, 'Why, sir, by the living God, I have not yet commenced to fight.' "—Hubbard.

OLIVER CROMWELL, Puritan reformer and Lord Protector of England, was born at Huntingdon, England. He entered Cambridge University in 1616. He studied law for a time in London, and on becoming of age married Elizabeth Bourchier, daughter of a wealthy London merchant. He was elected to the Parliament of 1628, where his only recorded speech is directed against the opponents of Puritanism. When the Civil War broke out in 1642, Cromwell had the backing of Parliament, and commanded a troop of horse, which came to be famous as "Cromwell's Ironsides." At the Battle of Marston Moor (1644) he commanded the Parliamentary troop whose final charge won the day. This performance was repeated at Naseby, the last battle of the First Civil War, 1645. In the Second Civil War Cromwell routed a greatly superior force in a three days' battle near Preston, which sealed the fate of King Charles I, who was executed January 30, 1649. Heading a military invasion of Ireland in that year, Cromwell ordered the massacre of the garrison of 2,800 men at Drogheda. Back in England he defeated a Scotch army at Dunbar in 1650, and another, commanded by Charles II, at Worcester. This marked the end of armed resistance to his rule. On December 16, 1653, Cromwell was constitutionally proclaimed Lord Protector.

❖ ❖ ❖

Cromwell is an example of the man who believes he has a special work to do in the world and allows nothing to stand in his way of doing it. As a militant reformer, he dreamt only of things that should or would come to pass through his agency. "Trust God, but keep your powder dry," was his motto.

SAMUEL ADAMS

Born 1722—Died 1813 Volume III—Page 79

CHIEF PROMOTER OF THE AMERICAN REVOLUTION

❖

"Samuel Adams kept out of sight and furthered his ends by pushing this man or that to the front at the right time. He was a master in that fine art of managing men and never letting them know they are managed." —Hubbard.

SAMUEL ADAMS, signer of the Declaration of Independence and an author of the American Revolution, was born in Boston, Massachusetts. His progenitors were of the New England aristocracy, originating with Henry Adams, a Puritan emigrant. Graduating from Harvard in 1740, he studied law for a while and then entered a counting-house preparatory to becoming a merchant on his own account. In business he seems to have been a failure, first as a brewer in partnership with his father. Their property was lost in a land-bank scheme abolished by an act of Parliament, which arbitrarily extended an English banking enactment to the Colonies. Meanwhile Samuel had become a power in town meetings, having strong and sincere democratic feelings and a genius for political management. His petition to King George apropos of the Townshend Acts of 1767, followed by a circular letter of appeal to the other Colonies, led directly to the Revolution. His activities in the cause of justice for the colonists were unceasing, and finally culminated in his direction of the Boston Tea Party in its work of December 17, 1773. When the port of Boston was closed and the charter of Massachusetts annulled in 1774, Adams carried through the measures for calling a Congress at Philadelphia, to which he was a delegate. In 1775 he and John Hancock were the only patriots excepted from amnesty by Governor-General Gage, whose military expedition to Lexington and Concord, resulting in the first battle of the Revolutionary War, was partly for the purpose of capturing Adams and Hancock. Adams was active in Congressional work throughout the Revolution.

❖ ❖ ❖

Samuel Adams had all the qualifications that go to make a shrewd silent partner or adviser, in a great enterprise. By keeping behind the scenes and directing others, he accomplished aims which could not have been accomplished had his own personality been constantly in evidence.

EDMUND BURKE

Born 1729—Died 1797 Volume VII—Page 159

EMINENT ANGLO-IRISH STATESMAN

❖

"*For thirty years Edmund Burke was a most prominent figure in English politics—no great measure could be passed without counting on him. His influence held dishonesty in check, and made oppression pause.*" —Hubbard.

EDMUND BURKE was born in Dublin, where his father was a successful attorney-at-law. Graduating from Trinity College, Dublin, he proceeded to London to pursue his legal studies in the Middle Temple. His tastes were more literary than legal, however, and he turned essayist, first publishing anonymously his celebrated *Vindication of Natural Society*, 1756. In the same year appeared his well-known essay, *On the Sublime and Beautiful*, which was praised by Johnson and Lessing. It gained him the friendship of such men as Garrick, Sir Joshua Reynolds, Lord Lyttleton, Goldsmith, Hume and Dr. Johnson. *An Account of the European Settlements in America* added to his literary reputation, and Burke was appointed private secretary to the Secretary for Ireland. This post he resigned at the end of two years, returned to London and became private secretary to Prime Minister Rockingham, at the same time entering Parliament. His eloquence made him "the first man in the Commons" over a period extending without intermission to 1794. During his Parliamentary career Burke rendered more important service to the cause of humanity than any other man of his time in Europe: among other things he prepared the way for the abolition of the slave-trade, curbed the exploitation of India, sought to prevent the American Revolution by dealing squarely with the Colonies. His *Reflections on the Revolution in France* provoked Thomas Paine to write *The Rights of Man*.

❖ ❖ ❖

Edmund Burke never undertook an important speech or action without being prepared. One never knows when he is going to be called upon to do something that may determine his entire future career. But, as the Little Journey to Burke brings out, the only insurance of success in any undertaking is to be prepared beforehand.

GEORGE WASHINGTON

Born 1732—Died 1799 Volume III—Page 5

FIRST PRESIDENT OF THE UNITED STATES

❖

"*We know Washington as well as it is possible to know any man. We know him better than the people who lived in the same house with him; and we find him human, splendidly human . . . a man to whom we pay the tribute of affection.*"—Hubbard.

GEORGE WASHINGTON, commander-in-chief of the Continental forces in the Revolutionary War and first President of the United States, was born in Westmoreland County, Virginia, the oldest son of Augustine Washington by his second wife, Mary Ball. Soon after his birth his parents removed to a farm near Fredericksburg. On the death of his father in 1743 George inherited the farm. Such formal schooling as he received was completed by the time he was sixteen, when he was commissioned as a public surveyor. George inherited the celebrated Mount Vernon property from his brother, Lawrence Washington, in 1752. His career as a Virginia planter was interrupted by the war with the French and Indians, in which Washington rendered distinguished service as an aide to the British General, Braddock. In 1759 he married Mrs. Martha Custis, a young and wealthy widow with two children. His capable management of their combined estates made him one of the wealthiest men in the Colonies at the outbreak of the Revolution. Chosen in 1775 to lead the American armies, it was largely through his generalship that the war for Independence was won. Washington was president of the Convention of 1787 which framed the Constitution, and was unanimously chosen first President of the Republic, taking the oath of office April 30, 1789. After serving two terms he declined a third, and on September 19, 1796, issued his Farewell Address to the country he had been so largely instrumental in forming almost out of chaos.

❖ ❖ ❖

The success of Washington as a business man, no less than as a soldier and statesman, was based upon character. The Father of His Country was no mysterious genius working in secret. He used no tricks, but won a great place in the world by being ready for every successive undertaking as it developed.

THOMAS PAINE

Born 1737—Died 1809 Volume IX—Page 157

FIRST AMERICAN REFORMER

❖

"The genius of Paine was a flower that blossomed slowly. But life is a sequence, and the man who does great work has been in training for it. Paine knew no more about what he was getting ready for than did Franklin, to whom he listened one whole evening, and then said, 'What he is I can at least in part become.'"—Hubbard.

THOMAS PAINE, who inspired the Declaration of Independence and whose writings were largely responsible for the success of the American Revolution, was born at Thetford, England, the son of a Quaker staymaker. He himself was a staymaker, then an exciseman. In 1774 he emigrated to America with letters of introduction from Benjamin Franklin, whom he had met and favorably impressed in London. Arriving in Philadelphia, he became editor of the *Pennsylvania Magazine*. Early in 1776 he published his famous pamphlet, *Common Sense*, in which he argued that the American Colonies should "become independent of the British Crown." Paine enlisted in the Continental Army, and his military experience prompted him to write *The Crisis*, which was widely read and had a powerful influence over the people. As the pamphlets appeared from time to time, 1776-1783, Washington had them read at the head of his regiments. In 1781 Paine was on a mission to France which obtained for the United States "2,500,000 livres in silver, and a ship laden with clothing and military stores." At Washington's suggestion Congress granted Paine $800 on condition that he use his pen to support the American cause. Other substantial grants were made by individual States. In 1792 Paine was a member of the French Convention, opposed the execution of Louis XVI, was thrown into prison, and wrote *The Age of Reason*, his famous exposition of Deism, which cost him the esteem of the orthodox in both hemispheres.

❖ ❖ ❖

If you have convictions and are afraid to express them, you will learn a lesson from Thomas Paine. Every once in a while conditions arise that make it necessary for one to come to a decision in matters involving a moral principle or standard of character. The Little Journey teaches the importance of honest thinking—of having the courage of one's convictions.

THOMAS JEFFERSON

Born 1743—Died 1826 Volume III—Page 55

AUTHOR OF THE DECLARATION OF INDEPENDENCE

❖

"Jefferson realized that the 'United States' with England as a sole pattern was not enough. A pivotal point! Yes, a pivotal point for Jefferson, America and the world; for Jefferson gave the rudder of the Ship of State such a turn to starboard that there was never again danger of her drifting on to aristocratic shoals."—Hubbard.

THOMAS JEFFERSON, author of the Declaration of Independence and third President of the United States, was born in Virginia. Graduating from William and Mary College, he studied law, and was admitted to the bar at twenty-four. Aside from his marriage, in 1772, to Martha Skelton, to whom he was singularly devoted, the most important event of his early manhood was the drafting in the Virginia House of Burgesses of *A Summary View of the Rights of British America*, which was widely circulated in England and which formed the basis of the Declaration of Independence. In 1775 Jefferson was a delegate to the second Continental Congress. His facility for writing was so well known that he was unanimously chosen to head the committee which drafted the Declaration. In 1783, as a member of Congress, Jefferson devised the decimal system of coinage. In 1789 he became Secretary of State in Washington's Cabinet. He became President in 1800, being the first President inaugurated in Washington City. The historic event of his first term was the purchase of Louisiana from the French for $15,000,000. On March 4, 1809, Jefferson retired from office and spent the remaining 17 years of his life on his 10,647-acre estate at Monticello.

❖ ❖ ❖

Hubbard hails Jefferson as the first man in history, who, while still having power in his grasp, was willing to trust the people. The author of the Declaration of Independence believed in the fundamental soundness of human nature. In this belief he conceived the principles of democratic government. Born to affluence himself, Jefferson sets what Hubbard calls an "almost ideal example" of simplicity, moderation and common-sense Americanism.

JEAN PAUL MARAT

Born 1744—Died 1793 Volume VII—Page 207

FRENCH REVOLUTIONARY LEADER

❖

"*Marat was full of the desire to educate—to make men think. He saw the needs of the poor . . . and observed how disease and death fasten themselves upon the ill-taught. Some one called him 'the people's friend.' The name stuck—he liked it.*"—Hubbard.

JEAN PAUL MARAT, one of the most extravagant, passionate and demagogical victor-victims of the French Reign of Terror, was born at Boudry, near Neufchâtel, Switzerland. In youth he mastered several languages, studied medicine at Bordeaux and Paris, and subsequently practiced for a time in London. Returning to Paris, in 1777, he became a veterinary surgeon. On the outbreak of the Revolution he at once gained prominence through his extreme radicalism. Indeed, his violence caused an order for his arrest in 1790, but he succeeded in evading capture; and Danton, who had found Marat useful in planning the attack on the Tuileries, made him a member of the Commune of Paris. It was his influence largely which led to the cruelties and massacres of 1792, amid which Marat was elected a member of the Convention. He was insistent upon executing Louis XVI swiftly, and in his *Journal de la République* he called upon the people to slay 200,000 royalist adherents. In 1793 Marat was tried before the Revolutionary Tribunal on the charge of fomenting sedition, but was acquitted. On July 13 of that year he was stabbed in his own house by Charlotte Corday.

❖ ❖ ❖

Courage and devotion to a cause were the outstanding characteristics of Marat. Such was his moral courage that Marat was as zealous in denouncing his fellow radicals on occasion as he was his enemies. The result was his enormous popularity with the people whose cause he championed.

JOHN JAY

Born 1745—Died 1829 Volume III—Page 231

FIRST CHIEF JUSTICE OF THE U. S. SUPREME COURT

❖

"No one has ever made the claim that Jay possessed genius. He had something which is better, though, for most of the affairs of life, and that is commonsense. . . . He was the average man who has trained and educated and made the best use of every faculty and every opportunity."
—Hubbard.

JOHN JAY, the first Chief Justice of the United States Supreme Court and negotiator of the Jay Treaty of 1794 with England, was born in New York City. Graduating from King's College (now Columbia University) in 1764, he studied law and was admitted to the bar four years later. His marriage, in 1774, to the daughter of William Livingston, first Governor of New Jersey, allied him with one of the most influential Whig families in the Colonies. In that year he was a delegate to the first Continental Congress and a member of the committee appointed "to state the rights of the Colonies in general." In 1776 he was chosen a member of the Provincial Congress of New York, by which body he was called away in May from the Continental Congress at Philadelphia, thus failing to become a signer of the Declaration of Independence. Subsequently he succeeded Henry Laurens as president of the Congress, and in 1782 joined Benjamin Franklin at Paris in negotiating the Treaty of Peace with Great Britain. Returning to America Jay became Secretary for Foreign Affairs under the Confederation, and upon the organization of the Federal Government was given his choice of all the public offices to be filled by President Washington. He chose to be Chief Justice of the Supreme Court, a position he filled with marked dignity and ability.

❖ ❖ ❖

Hubbard writes of John Jay as an average man who rose high in the world because of his thoroughness and trustworthiness. He won the confidence and esteem of men of influence with whom he came in contact and made the relationship mutually profitable. Here is the type of man who attempts nothing beyond his proven power to do successfully.

WILLIAM GODWIN

Born 1756—Died 1836 Volume XIII—Page 83

A GREAT POLITICAL HISTORIAN

❖

"*Godwin believed in the perfectibility of the race, and proved that man's career has been a constant movement forward. That is, there never was a 'Fall of Man.' Man has always fallen upward.*"—Hubbard.

WILLIAM GODWIN was born at Wisbeach, Cambridgeshire, England, and in his early manhood was a Protestant minister. Subsequently he became an agnostic. After a *Life of Chatham* (1783) and *Sketches of History in Six Sermons* (1784), he published the famous *Enquiry Concerning Political Justice* (1793), in which were presented the most radical theories of French philosophy on morals and government. By this work he is best known. It was followed by *The Adventures of Caleb Williams* (1794), a remarkable novel, intended to illustrate the political views advanced in the *Political Justice* and by *The Enquirer* (1797), a collection of essays on morals and politics. In 1796 Godwin formed an alliance with Mary Wollstonecraft. After some months they yielded so far to custom as to be married. His wife died a short time after, in giving birth to a daughter, the future wife of the poet Shelley. In 1799 Godwin published a successful romance entitled *Saint Leon*. In 1801 he married a Mrs. Clairmont, his next-door neighbor, who one day had accosted him from her balcony: "Is it possible that I behold the immortal Godwin?" A bookselling business, undertaken in 1805, involved him for years in difficulties, and in 1833 he was glad to accept the sinecure post of yeoman-usher of the Exchequer.

❖ ❖ ❖

William Godwin succeeded in developing and expressing an individuality of his own. He represents the type of man who is not content with being a copyist, but who must originate things, blaze a new trail. "All that the foremost of contemporary thinkers have written and said was suggested and touched upon by him," says Hubbard.

LORD NELSON

Born 1758—Died 1805 Volume XIII—Page 399

GREATEST OF ENGLISH ADMIRALS

❖

"When a ship mutinied, Nelson was placed in charge of it if he was within call; and the result was that he always won the absolute love and devotion of his men. . . . Nelson knew how to do three great things —how to fight, how to love, how to die."—Hubbard.

HORATIO (VISCOUNT) NELSON was born at Burnham-Thorpe, Norfolk, England. His father was an Episcopal clergyman and his mother a grand-niece of Sir Robert Walpole, the great English statesman. At the age of twelve the future "hero of Trafalgar" entered the British navy, and at nineteen was a second lieutenant. Two years later he became captain and saw varied service, particularly in the West Indies where he met the widow of a Dr. Josiah Nisbet, whom he married in 1787. In 1793, during the war with France, he was given command of the *Agamemnon*, which, together with his last ship, the *Victory*, is most closely associated with his career. In that year he met Sir William Hamilton and his wife, Lady Emma Hamilton, with whose name his own is coupled in history. While leading the marines in an attack on Corsica, Nelson lost the sight of his right eye. In the battle off Cape Saint Vincent, 1797, it was largely due to Nelson that a much larger Spanish fleet was totally defeated. In an attack on Santa Cruz, Teneriff Island, Nelson lost his right arm. In 1787 Nelson was given a pension of £2,000 a year after annihilating the French fleet at Abukir Bay. His relations with Lady Hamilton led to a separation from his wife in 1801. During the same year Nelson defeated the Danish fleet off Copenhagen. His greatest and last victory was over the French at Trafalgar, October 21, 1805. Mortally wounded, he died saying, "Thank God, I have done my duty."

❖ ❖ ❖

The Little Journey to Horatio Nelson reminds us that the courage which wins great victories is moral rather than physical. The hero of Trafalgar was so weak of body that as he early discovered, his only chance of success in any competitive enterprise was to substitute brain for brawn. The biggest prizes of life are the rewards that come through the exercise of intelligence such as Nelson applied.

WILLIAM PITT

Born 1759—Died 1806 Volume VII—Page 185

"ENGLAND'S GREATEST PRIME MINISTER"

❖

"The life of Pitt was a search for power . . . to dictate the policy of a great nation. All save honor was sacrificed to this end, and that the man was successful in his ambition, there is no dispute."—Hubbard.

WILLIAM PITT, often referred to as the younger Pitt to distinguish him from his father, William Pitt, first Earl of Chatham, was born at Hayes, England. His mother was a sister of an eminent statesman, George Grenville. Graduating from Cambridge University, Pitt entered Parliament in 1781, and at the age of twenty-three became Chancellor of the Exchequer. A year later King George III offered Pitt the Premiership, which for political reasons he declined. Presently he changed his mind, accepted it, dissolved Parliament and emerged triumphant from the popular election, being himself returned to Parliament from the University of Cambridge, for which he sat the rest of his life. As Prime Minister, Pitt ruled absolutely over the Cabinet, and was at once a royal favorite and popular idol. He was the first British statesman to attempt to put into practice the principles enunciated in 1776 by Adam Smith. In his persistent enmity toward Napoleon he was opposed by his great rival, Charles James Fox. When Napoleon had defeated Austria in Italy, while Russia became neutral, England was left to struggle with France alone. In 1801 Pitt resigned because the King refused to accept his Catholic emancipation measures. In 1804 Pitt again was Prime Minister, and though the naval victory of Trafalgar cheered him, the defeat of Austria and Russia at Austerlitz, 1805, proved his deathblow. He was buried in Westminster Abbey.

❖ ❖ ❖

So many sons have been overshadowed by distinguished fathers as to give a basis to the saying that great ability is seldom or never transmitted from father to son. Here is an exception. The Little Journey to the greater son of a great English Prime Minister offers encouragement to anyone who has a heritage to live up to. When, says Hubbard, young Pitt first spoke in Parliament, the members were amazed. "He's a chip off the old block," was said. "He's the old block itself," was decided.

EMPRESS JOSEPHINE

Born 1763—Died 1814 Volume II—Page 259

FIRST WIFE OF NAPOLEON I.

❖

"'*My dear, together we will win,' said Napoleon to Josephine; and later, 'I gain provinces, you win hearts.' Josephine worked for the glory of France and for her husband: she was diplomat and adviser. She placated enemies and made friends.*"—Hubbard.

MARIE JOSÉPHE ROSE TASCHER DE LA PAGERIE, first wife of Napoleon Bonaparte and Empress of the French, was born at Trois-Ilets, Martinique, and died at Malmaison, near Paris. Her father was captain of the port of Saint-Pierre. When about fifteen years of age, she went to France and became the wife of the Vicomte de Beauharnais, of which marriage were born Eugene, Viceroy of Italy, and Hortense, Queen of Holland, mother of the Emperor Napoleon III. Beauharnais was executed during the reign of Terror in 1794, and Josephine herself barely escaped the guillotine. She married Napoleon in 1796 and accompanied him during a part of his Italian campaign. She attracted around her the most brilliant society of France and contributed largely to the growing power of her husband. She regarded his exaltation to the throne, however, with fear, and from the day she became Empress (1804) apprehended the dissolution of their marriage, which had proved unfruitful. The marriage was in fact finally dissolved in 1809, and in the following year Napoleon married Maria Louisa of Austria. Josephine retained the title of Empress, corresponded with Bonaparte, and took the keenest interest in his doings. She died before his final defeat at Waterloo.

❖ ❖ ❖

Josephine, whom Napoleon made empress and later treated as an obstacle in the path of his ambition, is set forth in the Little Journey as an example of the incalculable influence a woman may have in advancing her husband's fortunes. Many a man, like Napoleon, owes his success in great part to his wife.

MADAME DE STAËL

Born 1766—Died 1817 Volume II—Page 163

A MAKER OF NAPOLEONIC HISTORY

❖

"*As a type her life is valuable, and in these pages that traverse the entire circle of feminine virtues and foibles Madame De Staël must have a place.*"—Hubbard.

ANNE LOUISE GERMAINE DE STAËL was the daughter of the distinguished French Minister of Finance, Jacques Necker. In 1786 she married Baron De Staël-Holstein, Swedish Minister to France. She sympathized with the cause of the French Revolutionists till the imprisonment of Louis XVI drove her to the opposite extreme. She abused her ministerial right of asylum, and, in fear of the consequences, left Paris before the massacres of September, 1792, going to Switzerland. Subsequently she returned to France and for nine years played at politics in the French capital. In 1788 she was amicably separated from her husband, and in 1803 she was banished by Napoleon whom she irritated with her biting epigrams. She went to Germany and formed the acquaintance of Goethe, Richter, Schiller and Schlegel, whose new school of philosophy she introduced into France. Her literary power was first revealed in the novel *Delphine* (1802), a half-autobiography of the "misunderstood woman," to be exploited later by George Sand. In 1810 she published *de l'Allemagne*, which Napoleon suppressed again, expelling her from France. Madame De Staël was a writer with great enthusiasms, faith in human progress and in democracy.

❖ ❖ ❖

Madame De Staël was one of the first of her sex to regard matrimony as the beginning, rather than the fulfillment, of a woman's career. She illustrates the influence a woman can exercise, if she will, in shaping thc course of civilization.

JOHN QUINCY ADAMS

Born 1767—Died 1848 Volume III—Page 127

THE MOST VERSATILE OF AMERICAN STATESMEN

❖

"Precocious, proud, firm, he made his way. It was a zigzag course, and the way was strewn with the flotsam and jetsam of wrecked parties and blighted hopes, but out of the wreckage John Quincy Adams always appeared calm, poised and serene."—Hubbard.

JOHN QUINCY ADAMS, sixth President of the United States and son of the second President, John Adams, was born at Quincy, Massachusetts. During his minority he accompanied his father on two missions to Europe, and for a time was private secretary to Francis Dana, American Minister to Russia. On the appointment of his father as Minister to England, the younger Adams returned home and entered Harvard from which he graduated in 1787. At twenty-seven, President Washington appointed him Minister to The Hague and later to Portugal, but before he had arrived at Lisbon his father had become President, and the son, upon the recommendation of Washington himself, was transferred to the more responsible post of Minister to Prussia. In 1803 he represented Massachusetts in the United States Senate. Later he was Minister to Russia, and was one of the five negotiators who concluded the Treaty of Ghent at the close of the War of 1812. Subsequently he was Minister to England and then Secretary of State in the Monroe Cabinet. By some historians John Quincy Adams is credited with the authorship of the Monroe Doctrine. In the Presidential campaign of 1824 the election was carried to the House of Representatives where the Adams and Henry Clay forces combined to elect Adams over his chief rival, Andrew Jackson. Four years later the tables were reversed, but, instead of retiring to private life, John Quincy Adams adopted the unprecedented course of returning to Washington as a member of the House of Representatives, in which capacity he served the nation from 1830 until his death.

❖ ❖ ❖

The Little Journey shows John Quincy Adams as a man who overcame the handicap of having a famous father and carved out a great career for himself. His father, John Adams, second President of the United States, lived to see his son sixth President. By serving seventeen years in Congress after leaving the White House, J. Q. Adams set a historic example.

HENRY CLAY

Born 1777—Died 1852 Volume III—Page 209

"THE GREAT PACIFICATOR"

❖

"Clay was a great statesman—one of the greatest this country has produced, and as a patriot no man was ever more loyal. It was America with him first and always. His reputation, his fortune, his life, his all, belonged to America."—Hubbard.

HENRY CLAY who, from his statesmanly skill in devising compromises, is known to history as the Great Pacificator, was born in a neighborhood called "The Slashes," in Hanover County, Virginia. His father, a Baptist minister in humble circumstances, died when Henry was four years old; and his mother, a woman of forcible character, eventually married again. Through his stepfather young Clay secured a court clerkship and attracted the notice of Chancellor Wythe, who had been the teacher of Jefferson and John Marshall. This contact did much to shape and develop Henry Clay, who had received almost no schooling and never studied regularly. Clay was admitted to the Virginia bar at twenty, and soon afterward located in Lexington, Ky. He rose rapidly in his profession, being sent to the United States Senate at twenty-nine. At thirty-four he was Speaker of the House of Representatives, and is credited with practically forcing the War of 1812 with England. Although it failed of securing anything that Clay had demanded of England, he was made a member of the commission which signed the Treaty of Ghent in 1814. Clay presided over several subsequent Congresses and was instrumental in bringing about the passage of the Missouri Compromise of 1820. Several times he was a prominent candidate for the Presidency.

❖ ❖ ❖

Clay, like Lincoln, who regarded him as "the beau ideal statesman," is an illustration of what a poor boy, with no educational advantages, nor opportunity for regular study, can accomplish. He developed qualities within himself that account mainly for his success. Working to preserve the Union at a critical period, Clay earned his popular sobriquet. As Hubbard brings out in the Little Journey, Clay staked his all on America and made pure patriotism a paying investment.

ELIZABETH FRY

Born 1780—Died 1845 Volume II—Page 189

PIONEER PRISON REFORMER

❖

"*Elizabeth Fry [first] asked that the word asylum be dropped, and home or hospital used instead. . . . In penology nothing has been added to her philosophy, and we have as yet not nearly carried out her suggestions.*"—Hubbard.

ELIZABETH FRY was born of Quaker parentage at Earlham, Norfolk, England, her maiden name being Gurney. As a child of fifteen she became deeply interested in the house of correction at Norwich. In 1813 she first became practically engaged in prison reform, and turned her attention to the condition of women prisoners at Newgate. Under her leadership an association was formed in 1817 for the improvement of these unfortunates, and did much to better their condition materially and morally. Mrs. Fry also joined in the movement to induce the Government to make proper regulations for the transportation of convicts to New South Wales, and to provide employment for them there. She founded prison associations throughout England, and contributed materially to prison reform in the principal countries of Europe. It is remarkable that the mother of a large family herself should have had the inclination and found the time to accomplish what Elizabeth Fry did in public welfare work. Through her influence libraries were begun in the naval hospitals and the coastguard stations of the British Isles and Bibles were supplied to them. She was peculiarly gifted for the difficult service she rendered through her sympathy, swift insight, tact and charm of manner.

❖ ❖ ❖

Without neglecting her home and family of twelve children, Elizabeth Fry succeeded in bringing about prison reforms in England and Europe that still make her an example to humanitarians. This Little Journey makes plain the fact that it is the busy woman as well as man, who finds time to help others and make the world a better place to live in.

DANIEL WEBSTER

Born 1782—Died 1852 Volume III—Page 185

AMERICAN STATESMAN AND ORATOR

"Webster believed in America. Into the minds of countless men he infused his own splendid patriotism. . . . How much the growing greatness of our country is due to the magic of his words and the eloquence of his inspired presence no man can compute."—Hubbard.

DANIEL WEBSTER was born in Salisbury (now Franklin) New Hampshire, Graduating from Dartmouth College in 1801, he studied law and was admitted to the bar in 1805. From 1813 to 1817 Webster represented New Hampshire in Congress, after which he built up a law practice in Boston that paid him $20,000 a year. With ample means and a high standing at the bar, Webster delivered a series of commemorative orations that made his name known nationally. The Plymouth (1820) and the Bunker Hill (1825) speeches were the best of them. He also appeared in many famous law cases, among them the Dartmouth College and the Girard Will cases. In 1827 Webster was elected to the United States Senate. Three years later his fame as an orator culminated in his great debate with Senator Robert Y. Hayne, of South Carolina, on the nature of the Union and the right of nullification. In this epoch-making oration Webster upheld the nationalist view of the Union and denied the right of a State to nullify any Federal statute. He became Secretary of State in the first Harrison Cabinet, retaining the post under President Tyler. In 1844 he reentered the Senate, devoting his efforts to preserve the Union and maintain peace between the North and South by means of compromise. His last great speech and one of the most notable of his life was delivered in the Senate, March 7, 1850, on the Compromise Measures of 1850, in which he rebuked the North for agitating the slavery question and for violating the Fugitive Slave Law.

❖ ❖ ❖

Daniel Webster was given an education only because he was too weak as a boy to do hard manual labor. It was the necessity of making the most of his natural abilities, or, as Hubbard says, "of getting all his goods in the front window," that resulted in his becoming one of the greatest orators that ever lived.

Thomas B. Macaulay

Born 1800—Died 1859 Volume V—Page 173

English Historian-Statesman

❖

"If ever a writing man had success tied to the leg of his easy chair, that man was Macaulay. . . . He made a reputation as a writer by his first article, and after his maiden speech [in Parliament] all London chanted his praises as an orator."—Hubbard.

THOMAS BABINGTON MACAULAY was born at Rothley Temple Leicestershire, England. He early evidenced extraordinary mentality and at Cambridge University acquired a reputation both as a scholar and a debater. In 1825, shortly after his graduation, he published in the Edinburgh *Review* his famous essay on Milton. He was called to the bar, but found the practice of law uncongenial, and through political influence, in 1830, he was elected to the House of Commons. In 1834 he went to India as a member of the Supreme Council. Four years later he returned to England and was returned to Parliament from the city of Edinburgh. In 1842 were published his martial ballads, *Lays of Ancient Rome*, and in 1843 three volumes of *Essays*. In contrast to his growing literary popularity, Macaulay lost his seat in Parliament, in 1847, through his too-zealous advocacy of religious toleration. He then wrote his great *History of England from the Accession of James II.* The first two volumes of the work appeared in 1848 and its reception rivaled that of the novels of Sir Walter Scott. Macaulay was elected lord rector of the University of Glasgow, declined a Cabinet post and, in 1855, published the third and fourth volumes of his *History*. In the United States their sale was comparable to that of the Bible. His premature death in his sixtieth year left his great *History* unfinished, though enough was done to constitute a monumental work.

❖ ❖ ❖

Macaulay achieved distinction as an orator, historian, essayist and administrator. Honors sought him continually. Macaulay was never idle. As Hubbard states, "If you want a piece of work well and thoroughly done, pick a busy man to do it."

Benjamin Disraeli

Born 1804—Died 1881 Volume V—Page 319

A Great Jewish Statesman

❖

"Any man who shows himself to be strong has friends—people wish to attach themselves to such a one. Disraeli showed himself strong in that he held no resentment. . . . He was in the front of every fight—crossed swords with the strongest men of his age."—Hubbard.

BENJAMIN DISRAELI, Earl of Beaconsfield, was born and died in London, England. He first became famous as a novelist, before entering Parliament in 1837. His maiden speech excited ridicule, which prompted Disraeli to exclaim, "I shall sit down now, but the time is coming when you will hear me." Bearing out the prophecy, in 1852, he became Chancellor of the Exchequer. Between that time and 1866 he was in eclipse politically, but his talents, spirit and persistency were so great that he won admiration even from his opponents. In 1868 he became Prime Minister, and held the office again from 1874 to 1880. During that period England acquired the Suez Canal and the Queen of England became Empress of India. Disraeli stopped the Russian advance on Constantinople in 1878 by sending a British fleet to the Dardanelles and an army to Malta. In Africa the Transvaal was annexed and the Zulu power broken. In 1880, however, the Disraeli Ministry was overthrown, the poor health of the Premier having meanwhile caused him to withdraw from the leadership of the House of Commons. Two years previously he had entered the House of Lords as the Earl of Beaconsfield. His private life was above reproach. Marrying a rich widow much older than himself, in 1839, he found in her "the perfect wife," and when she died, in 1868, he felt that "he had no longer a home."

❖ ❖ ❖

Self-confidence was the main asset of Disraeli in his rise to power as one of the greatest English Prime Ministers. Few men have contended with heavier odds or have had more discouragements to overcome. Such was his confidence in himself, however, that he assured a mocking House of Commons that he would some day dominate it. History furnishes no better example of patience on the part of conscious ability than is recorded in the Little Journey to Disraeli.

GARIBALDI

Born 1807—Died 1882 Volume IX—Page 93

A GREAT LIBERATOR

❖

"Garibaldi won every one he desired to win. His power over men was superb. . . . He knew that only through liberty can men progress and grow; and that great and beautiful work can be done only by a free and happy people."—Hubbard.

GIUSEPPE GARIBALDI, adventurer, patriot and "father of modern Italy," was born at Nice and died at Caprera, Italy. Meeting Mazzini in 1833, he developed an unquenchable hatred of despotism and spent some years in South America rehearsing for the great role he was to play in Italian politics. He also lived in exile for a time on Staten Island, New York, supporting himself by making candles in a factory. Returning to Italy in 1860, Garibaldi assembled a force of 1,070 patriots with which he routed 3,600 Neapolitan troops preparatory to capturing Palermo and taking control of Sicily in the name of Victor Emmanuel. Subsequently his forces occupied Salerno, and Garibaldi entered Naples unattended by a military escort to prove to Europe that he was a liberator, not a conqueror. In 1862 he raised a force of volunteers at Palermo, invaded Calabria and marched upon Rome, which he believed must be wrested from the Pope before the unity of Italy could be accomplished. Frustrated in this by Victor Emmanuel himself, he persisted in organizing an open invasion of the Papal States and suffered an overwhelming defeat at Mentana, in 1867, when he was made a prisoner and interned at Caprera. In the neighborhood a man-of-war was stationed to prevent his escape. It was there that he died.

❖ ❖ ❖

Garibaldi typifies the man who achieves a great success without being aware of the fact. Surviving sixty-seven battles fought in the cause of liberty, he was influential in bringing about a united Italy, but regarded his work half done because he aimed to make Italy a Republic. Garibaldi proves that it is better to have a great ambition and partly fulfill it than to be satisfied with a small achievement.

ABRAHAM LINCOLN

Born 1809—Died 1865 Volume III—Page 279

THE GREAT EMANCIPATOR

❖

"Lincoln sought to lose himself among the people. And to the people at length he gave his time, his talents, his love, his life. . . . The memory of his gentleness, his patience, his firm faith, and his great and loving heart is the priceless heritage of a united land."—Hubbard.

ABRAHAM LINCOLN, sixteenth President of the United States, was born in Hardin County, Kentucky. He was descended from a Quaker family of English origin. His father, Thomas, settled with his family in Indiana in 1816, and in Illinois in 1830. His mother was Nancy Hanks, Thomas Lincoln's first wife. After gaining a precarious living as a farm laborer, salesman, merchant and surveyor by turns, Lincoln was admitted to the Illinois bar in 1836 and began practicing law in Springfield. As a result of the national attention attracted by his debates with Stephen A. Douglas in 1858, in which he took a pronounced stand against slavery, Lincoln was nominated and elected President in 1860. His inauguration was the signal for the secession, one after another, of the slave States of the South and for the organization of the Confederacy. Hostilities began with an attack by the South Carolina Secessionalists on the Federal troops at Fort Sumter, April 12, 1861. The fort surrendered the next day. On April 15 the President issued a call for 75,000 volunteers, and the control of events passed from the cabinet to the camp. Lincoln proclaimed a blockade of the Southern ports, April 19, 1861; and on September 22, 1862, issued a proclamation emancipating all slaves in States which should be in rebellion January 1, 1865. He was occupied with plans for the reconstruction of the South when he was assassinated.

❖ ❖ ❖

Hubbard himself was a product of the "Lincoln country" in central Illinois, and he saw the great Emancipator as a neighborly, as well as national, example of the self-made, self-educated American. It was the Lincoln of local tradition who instilled in Hubbard as a boy the reading habit and the desire for self-improvement. This Lincoln "influence" is evidenced throughout the Little Journey to the martyr President.

WILLIAM E. GLADSTONE

Born 1809—Died 1898 Volume I—Page 103

THE "GRAND OLD MAN" OF BRITISH POLITICS

❖

"The influence of Gladstone has been of untold value to England. His ideals for national action were high. To the material prosperity of the country he added millions; he made education popular, and schooling easy; his policy in the main was such as to command the admiration of the good and great."—Hubbard.

WILLIAM EWART GLADSTONE was born in the same year that Abraham Lincoln and Charles Darwin were born, and he outlived them both. His parentage was Scotch on both sides, though his father was a wealthy Liverpool merchant, a baronet and member of Parliament from the Lancashire metropolis. Entering Parliament almost immediately after graduating from Oxford in 1832, he delivered his maiden speech in 1833. In 1852 Gladstone first came into conflict with his great rival Disraeli, whose budget he completely demolished in favor of one of his own. As Chancellor of the Exchequer in 1860-61, Gladstone issued budgets that were marvels of financial statesmanship. He allied himself with John Bright and Richard Cobden in bringing about the repeal of the Corn Laws, and won a complete victory over the House of Lords in 1861, after it had defeated his measure for the abolition of a tax on paper. This was a triumph for popular education and a free press, inaugurating the new era of cheap newspapers in England. Becoming leader of the Liberal Party in 1867, Gladstone succeeded Disraeli as Prime Minister and remained in power until 1874. In 1880, 1886 and 1892 successively he was Prime Minister. Weary of the tumults of Parliamentary life, he resigned from office in 1894.

❖ ❖ ❖

What most impressed Hubbard in Gladstone was his lifelong mental vigor and enthusiasm, attributed to his habit of interesting himself in a great variety of things. To keep an ever fresh outlook is the lesson to be derived from the Little Journey to Gladstone.

CHARLES STEWART PARNELL

Born 1846—Died 1891 Volume XIII—Page 175

A GREAT IRISH REVOLUTIONARY LEADER

❖

"Parnell seemed filled with the idea, from the days of his youth, that he had a mission—he was to lead his people out of captivity. This oneness of purpose made itself felt in the House of Commons from his first entrance."—Hubbard.

CHARLES STEWART PARNELL was born at Avondale, County of Wicklow, Ireland, of an old Protestant family. His mother was the daughter of Rear Admiral Charles Stewart of the United States Navy. In 1877 Parnell and Joseph Biggar, another Irish leader, united the forces of opposition in a compact body of Nationalists, whose object was Home Rule for Ireland and the restoration of the Irish Parliament. In support of this policy Parnell had behind him the Fenians of Ireland and America and the Land League, which he helped organize in 1879, and of which he was the first president. He fought his Parliamentary battles with singular tenacity and persistence, against the bitter opposition of both the great English parties. To strengthen his cause financially, Parnell visited America in 1879-80 and raised large sums by popular subscription. His power in English politics became formidable and his prestige grew with the passing years. In 1887 he was accused of palliating the murder of the English Under-Secretary for Ireland, but triumphantly exonerated himself and recovered heavy damages for libel from the London *Times*. Subsequently he became involved in a scandal with the wife of a Captain O'Shea, who secured a divorce, naming Parnell as co-respondent. Although Parnell and Kitty O'Shea married, the affair ruined him politically and hastened his death a few months later.

❖ ❖ ❖

Parnell typifies the man whose whole life is given over to the accomplishment of one purpose. In his case it was to free Ireland from English domination. To have one big idea and to carry it out, instead of wasting time and energy on trivialities, is the point made in this Little Journey.

BOOK THREE

❖

LITERATURE, ORATORY, ROMANCE

DANTE ALIGHIERI

Born 1265—Died 1321 Volume XIII—Page 111

THE GREATEST POET OF ITALY

"If it be true that much of modern Christianity traces to Dante, it is no less true that he is the father of modern literature. He is the first writer of worth to emerge out of that night of darkness called the Middle Ages."—Hubbard.

❖

DANTE (originally Durante) ALIGHIERI was born in Florence, Italy, the son of a lawyer or jurist of some prominence. Of his mother nothing is known except that her name was Bella. She died when he was ten years of age, and he was brought up by a step-mother. Of his boyhood and education we know little beyond his own statement that he had "taught himself the art of bringing words into verse." The most significant event of his early youth, and the one fraught with most enduring consequences, was his meeting with the Beatrice afterwards celebrated in his poems, and believed, upon the authority of Boccaccio, to have been the daughter of one Folco Portinari. Beatrice died in 1290, and a year or more later Dante married Gemma Donati, who bore him two sons and two daughters, one of whom was named Beatrice. Dante saw military service, taking part in the Arezzo invasion of 1289, and the capture of the fortress of Caprona by Florentine troops. In 1300 he was chosen one of the six Priors of Florence, but was banished two years later and was long in exile. In 1317 he made his permanent home at Ravenna, where he passed his last years, busied with the completion of his great epic, *The Divine Comedy*, and surrounded by his children and friends at the time of his death. For fear of theft, his remains were hidden, and their resting place remained a secret down to 1865, since which time they have been jealously guarded by Ravenna.

❖ ❖ ❖

The Little Journey to Dante vividly portrays the truth that without human love there would be no such thing as poetry. It was his ideal love for a woman, Beatrice, that made the author of *The Divine Comedy* the great poet that he was. Back of every great imaginative work may be found something of the same idealism.

PETRARCH

Born 1304—Died 1374 Volume XIII—Page 209

A GREAT LYRIC POET OF THE MIDDLE AGES

"*Petrarch . . . was at home in every phase of society; his creations were greater than his poems; and as a diplomat, wise, discreet, sincere, loyal to his own, he was almost the equal of our own Doctor Franklin.*" —Hubbard.

❖

FRANCESCO PETRARCH (Italian Petrarca) was born at Arezzo, and died near Padua, Italy. At the time of his birth his father, along with the poet Dante, was an exile from Florence. Petrarch remembered seeing Dante in his childhood. The family went to Avignon, France, in 1313, and when about fourteen years old the embryonic poet went to the French University of Montpellier, remaining there four years. In 1327 he first saw the Laura of his sonnets. There have been many theories as to her identity. The one accepted by Hubbard is that she was the wife of one Hugh de Sade, to whom she had borne eleven children at the time of her death in 1348. The relations between Petrarch and Laura are believed to have been platonic. Petrarch was made the Canon of Lombez, at the foot of the Pyrenees, in 1335. In 1337 he bought a house at Vaucluse, near Avignon, to which he retired and where he did most of his best work. Three years afterwards he was called simultaneously to Rome and to Paris to be crowned as poet laureate. He received the laurel crown at Rome in 1341. In 1347 he built a house at Parma, and later settled at Milan. He was patronized by nobles and ecclesiastics, and was employed on various important diplomatic missions. In 1362 he removed to Padua, where he had held a canonry since 1347, and to Venice in the same year, where he met his friend Boccaccio for the last time. Petrarch prided himself much more on his Latin than on his Italian writings, by which he is best remembered.

❖ ❖ ❖

Hubbard makes the Little Journey to Petrarch as the first great poet on record who was equally proficient as a man of affairs, churchman, diplomat, statesman and as a lover. His all-round success is attributed to his ability to see men as they were, and not through the eyes of exaggeration. He realized his own worth and his example is one that will help others today, as it did in his own time, to realize theirs.

WILLIAM SHAKESPEARE

Born 1564—Died 1616 Volume I—Page 301

THE GREATEST ENGLISH DRAMATIST

"His name is honored in every school or college of earth where books are prized. There is no scholar in any clime who is not his debtor. . . . Why a monument to Shakespeare? He is his own monument and England is its pedestal."—Hubbard.

❖

WILLIAM SHAKESPEARE was born at Stratford-upon-Avon, in Warwickshire, England. Of a family of four sons and four daughters, he was the third child and eldest son. His father was a glover, and his mother, Mary Arden, the daughter of a Warwickshire farmer. Where or how Shakespeare was educated is not known, but there is no record of his attending any college. In 1582 he procured a license to marry Anne Hathaway of Shottery, who survived him seven years and who bore him three children. About 1587 Shakespeare went to London to seek his fortune and became by turns an actor, dramatist and play-producer. His son, Hamnet, having died in 1596, Shakespeare went for a short time to Stratford and bought a residence known as New Place. The Globe Theater, of which he was a proprietor, was opened in London in 1599, after which time his plays were first produced there. In 1610 he retired from the theater, and was living in Stratford in 1611. In 1613 he bought a house near Blackfriars Theater, London, in which he also had a proprietary interest, and about the same time he is believed to have disposed of his theatrical properties. Little is known of his life in Stratford after his retirement from the stage, but his name appears in documents until 1615. On February 10, 1616, his daughter, Judith, married Thomas Quiney, a vintner. Shakespeare died the following April.

❖ ❖ ❖

Shakespeare exposes three fallacies. First, that only a man of college education can produce great literature. Shakespeare himself had little formal schooling. Second, that artistic genius and business ability do not go together. Shakespeare was an eminently successful play-producer as well as writer. Third, that travel is necessary to such broad culture and understanding as Shakespeare possessed. The great dramatist was never out of his native England.

FÉNELON

Born 1651—Died 1715 Volume XIII—Page 313

A Romantic Churchman

"The nature of the man was to defend the accused person; this was evidenced by his defense of the Huguenots, when he lifted up his voice for their liberty at a time when religious liberty was unknown."—Hubbard.

❖

FRANÇOIS DE SALIGNAC DE LA MOTHE-FÉNELON was born in the chateau of his ancestors at Dordogne, France. He was equally celebrated as a prelate, orator and author. His name is romantically associated with that of Madame Guyon, a noble French churchwoman, whom he defended to the cost of his clerical reputation. Graduating with highest honors from the Jesuit College Du Plessis in Paris, at twenty Fénelon entered the Seminary of Saint Sulpice, and in 1675 received holy orders. Three years later he was made director of the Nouvelles Catholiques, a community of women founded for the purpose of strengthening female converts in the faith and instructing those who desired to abandon heresy. At this time he wrote his book, *On the Education of a Daughter*, at first privately circulated, but which was published in 1681 in response to a public demand. It has been called an anticipatory condemnation of Rousseau's *Emile*. In 1689 Louis XIV appointed Fénelon to the highly responsible post of preceptor to his grandson, the young Duke of Burgundy, heir in prospect to the French throne. In this position Fénelon showed himself a great practical educator, and composed text-books that are still popular in educational use. In 1695 he became Archbishop of Cambrai, and during this period began his association with Madame Guyon. His last years were spent at Cambrai, where he died.

❖ ❖ ❖

Declared to be the "greatest and most saintly man of his time," the French Archbishop Fénelon illustrates, by contrast, the value of using prudence in any undertaking that involves danger. Generously defending Madame Guyon on the charge of preaching too liberal doctrines, the great scholar-prelate brought disaster on both of them.

JONATHAN SWIFT

Born 1667—Died 1745 Volume I—Page 143

THE GREATEST OF ENGLISH SATIRISTS

"The positive elements in Swift's character make him a most interesting subject to men and women who are yet on earth, for he was essentially of the earth earthy. And until we are shown that the earth is wholly bad, we shall find much to amuse, much to instruct, much to admire, in Jonathan Swift."—Hubbard.

❖

JONATHAN SWIFT was born in Dublin, Ireland. He was of Yorkshire origin. Graduating from Trinity College, Dublin, in 1688, he went to England and found employment as secretary to the statesman and essayist, Sir William Temple. In 1694 he quarreled with his employer and returned to Ireland to seek ordination, obtaining the small living of Kilroot, near Belfast. Later he reëntered the employ of Temple, attracted probably by the presence in his household of Esther Johnson, subsequently immortalized as *Stella*. Irritated by his failure to gain recognition as a poet, Swift wrote *The Battle of the Books*, a burlesque of the controversy then raging over the relative merits of the ancients and moderns. He returned once more to Ireland, as secretary and chaplain to Lord Berkeley, later finding other church employment. In 1704 he published *The Tale of a Tub*, the most amusing of his satirical works, ridiculing many forms of pedantry in literature and religion. Six years later appeared the beginning of his *Journal to Stella*, for whom he had a deep affection and whom he may have married in 1716. Her only rival was Hester Vanhomrigh (called *Vanessa* by Swift), who hugged the chains to which Stella merely submitted. Both died, and by way of consolation for his loss Swift reached the summit of popularity with his *Drapier Letters*, followed by *Gulliver's Travels* (1726). Swift was buried in the same coffin with Stella in St. Patrick's Cathedral, Dublin, of which he was dean.

Dean Swift is depicted as a man who never got what he really wanted and most earnestly sought. Every time he was disappointed, however, he turned his failure into a success. It was his failure to be made a bishop, for instance, that led him to become a great writer of satire.

JOSEPH ADDISON

Born 1672—Died 1719 Volume V—Page 235

MODEL ENGLISH ESSAYIST

"Addison was a gentleman—the best example of a perfect gentleman that the history of English literature affords. And in letters it is much easier to find a genius than a gentleman."—Hubbard.

❖

JOSEPH ADDISON, son of an English clergyman, was born in Wiltshire, England. After attending the Charterhouse and other schools, he graduated from Oxford, where he was distinguished for the ease with which he wrote Latin verse. By 1697 he was receiving high compliments from Dryden, poet-laureate and arbiter of English literature at the time. A substantial pension enabled him to travel abroad to prepare himself for a diplomatic career. While in Italy he wrote the most successful of his poems, *The Letter*, followed by *The Campaign*, which so pleased the British ministry that the poet was given a lucrative government post. In 1709 he became associated with Sir Richard Steele as a contributor to the famous *Tatler*. Four years later his *Tragedy of Cato* scored an amazing dramatic success. It was translated into several languages; and the great Voltaire in France pronounced Addison superior to Shakespeare as a tragic poet. In 1716 Addison married the Dowager Duchess of Warwick, and in the following year was appointed Secretary of State. For this important political office he was not at all suited, and he resigned in 1718. His health had been declining for some time, and, after an illness of a few months, he died at Holland House, his wife's home in London, three years after what Thackeray calls "his splendid but dismal union." His literary monument is that series of sketches in the *Spectator*, of which Sir Roger de Coverley is the central figure and Sir Andrew Freeport and Will Honeycomb the lesser ones.

❖ ❖ ❖

In citing Addison as a "gentleman of letters," who did more than any one else of his time to make literature popular, Hubbard points to his success as a clean one achieved in a clean way.

SAMUEL JOHNSON

Born 1709—Died 1784 Volume V—Page 145

"THE GREAT LEXICOGRAPHER"

"*Behold this blundering giant, and you will see that the basis of his character was a great sincerity. He was honest—doggedly honest—and saw with flashing vision the thing that was; and thither he followed, crowding, pushing, knocking down whatsoever opinion or prejudice was in the way.*"—Hubbard.

❖

SAMUEL JOHNSON was born at Lichfield, England, the son of a bookseller. In addition to receiving a grammar-school education, he spent three years at Oxford, where he became known for his wide range of information and his mastery of Latin and Greek. In 1732 he was usher in a school at Market Bosworth, a position to which his nervousness rendered him particularly unsuited. He soon gave it up and became a contributor to the Birmingham *Journal*. While in Birmingham he met and married a widow twenty years his senior, whose small fortune enabled him to open a boarding school near Lichfield. Among his few pupils was David Garrick, who was to become the foremost actor-manager of the English stage. In 1737 Johnson and Garrick went fortune-seeking to London and suffered many privations. Eventually Johnson became a regular contributor to the *Gentleman's Magazine*, edited a set of Parliamentary debates and did various literary hack work. His poetic satire, *London*, placed him among the best followers of Pope. His reputation was further enhanced by his *Life of Richard Savage* (1744) and *The Vanity of Human Wishes* (1749), the finest of his poems. Garrick produced Johnson's tragedy, *Irene*, with fair success, and besides writing his *Rambler* and *Idler* essays Johnson edited a new *Dictionary of the English Language*, published in 1775. Meanwhile he wrote *Rasselas*, to pay his mother's funeral expenses. His literary career closed with the *Lives of the Poets*, the most admirable of his essays in both thought and style.

In the Little Journey to Samuel Johnson is illustrated a man who always had an ideal before him. As a rule, it was too high for him to attain, but he was never discouraged for long. In other words, it is better to aim high and accomplish an object now and then, than to aim low and be satisfied with mediocrity.

PATRICK HENRY

Born 1736—Died 1799 Volume VII—Page 277

FIRST GREAT AMERICAN ORATOR

"Patrick Henry could move men; he could mold their thoughts; he could convince them and bring them over to his way of thinking. . . . At once he took his place among the strong men of Virginia."—Hubbard.

❖

PATRICK HENRY was born in Hanover County, Virginia. His father was a native of Scotland. Patrick himself was unpromising as a scholar and in his early manhood showed no aptitude for business of any kind. But at intervals he read such books as he could find, and managed to gain a fair idea of Latin and Greek. Taking up the study of law, after a period of a month or six weeks of reading, he had the boldness to ask for a license to practice. This was granted in 1760, on condition that he would study longer before undertaking to practice. In 1763 he leapt into prominence, in a celebrated case known as the "Parsons' Cause," by an unexpectedly brilliant speech which established his reputation. In 1765 he became a member of the House of Burgesses and his fame was further extended by a speech in denunciation of the British Stamp Act. He continued his law practice, and though deficient in legal education, was wonderfully successful before juries. As a delegate to the first Continental Congress, he was hailed as the champion of constitutional liberty. Returning to Virginia, he delivered his famous "give me liberty or give me death" speech, and subsequently led the militia to a victory over trained British troops. He was Governor of Virginia from 1776 to 1779 and again from 1784 to 1786. In 1794 he declined a seat in the United States Senate, also the position of Secretary of State and the Chief Justiceship of the United States Supreme Court, tendered him by Washington. Elected to the House of Delegates in 1799, he did not live to take his seat.

❖ ❖ ❖

In the Little Journey to Patrick Henry is traced the development of a man who did not know his own powers until he was called upon to exert himself in an emergency. To some degree, this applies to everybody. The occasion reveals the man as ready or unready to rise to it.

MARY LAMB

Born 1764—Died 1847 Volume II—Page 215

SISTER AND COLLABORATOR OF CHARLES LAMB

"He who tells the tale of Charles and Mary Lamb's life must tell of a love that was an uplift to this brother and sister in childhood, that sustained them in the desolation of disaster, and was a saving solace even when every hope seemed gone."—Hubbard.

❖

MARY LAMB, like her brother, Charles, was a native of London, England. Her father was a law clerk in the employ of a wealthy barrister named Samuel Salt, whose death in 1792 left John Lamb without employment but with a small legacy. With this legacy, coupled with Charles's salary as a clerk at the India House, and whatever Mary could earn by needlework, in which she was proficient, the family retired from quarters in the Inner Temple to humble lodgings. In 1796 they resided in Little Queen Street, Holborn, where, becoming suddenly demented during an altercation with a servant girl, Mary Lamb snatched a knife from the dining-room table and stabbed her mother, who had interposed in the girl's behalf. Charles was himself present, and wrested the knife from his sister's hand. She was adjudged temporarily insane, and would ordinarily have been committed to an asylum; but her brother's guardianship was accepted by the authorities as an alternative. The devotion of the couple over a period of thirty-eight years is the most remarkable in the annals of literature. Mary remained subject to attacks of temporary aberration for the rest of her life. "We are very poor," writes Mary Lamb in 1804; and again in 1805, "It has been sad and heavy times with us lately." In 1807 Mary and Charles Lamb wrote their well-known *Tales from Shakespeare*, Mary making the version of the comedies, and Charles that of the tragedies. It was an immediate success, and yielded sixty guineas. Subsequently the brother and sister composed jointly two other juvenile works—*Mrs. Leicester's School* and *Poetry for Children.* Mary survived her brother thirteen years.

That Mary Lamb, guilty of matricide and haunted throughout her life by the specter of insanity, should have produced noble literature, is an example of what is possible in the way of human accomplishment.

JANE AUSTEN

Born 1775—Died 1817 Volume II—Page 237

PIONEER WOMAN NOVELIST

"*Jane Austen was a commonplace person. She swept, sewed, worked, and did the duty that lay nearest her. She wrote because she liked to, and because it gave pleasure to others. She wrote as well as she could. She had no thought of immortality.*"—Hubbard.

❖

JANE AUSTEN was born at Steventon, Hampshire, England. When a girl, Jane learned French and Italian, and, encouraged by her father, read widely in contemporary English literature. Throughout her life she was distinguished alike by good sense, sweetness of disposition and personal attractiveness. Her novels are remarkable for the truthfulness with which they portray the everyday life of middle class English people in her time. Sir Walter Scott said of her: "That young lady has talent for describing the involvements, feelings and characters of ordinary life, which is to me the most wonderful I ever met with. The big Bow-Wow strain I can do myself, like any now going; but the exquisite touch, which renders ordinary, commonplace things and characters interesting from the truth of the description and the sentiment, is denied to me." Miss Austen's first four novels—*Sense and Sensibility*, *Pride and Prejudice*, *Mansfield Park* and *Emma*—were published between 1811 and 1816. *Northanger Abbey* and *Persuasion* appeared posthumously in 1818. In 1801 Jane went with her family, consisting, in addition to her parents, of a sister and six brothers, to Bath, and after her father's death in 1805, removed to Southampton, and finally, in 1809, to Chawton near Winchester. She died at Winchester and was buried there in the cathedral.

❖ ❖ ❖

In the Little Journey to Jane Austen is pictured a woman who, as Hubbard says, "lived a beautiful, helpful life and produced great art, yet knew it not."

THOMAS CARLYLE

Born 1795—Died 1881 Volume I—Page 67

SCOTCH MASTER OF LETTERS

"*When Carlyle took time to bring the ponderous machinery of his intellect to bear on a theme, he saw it through and through. . . . In history he goes beyond the political and conventional—showing us the thought, the hope, the fear, the passion of the soul.*"—Hubbard.

THOMAS CARLYLE was born at Ecclefechan, Dumfriesshire, Scotland, Educated at Edinburgh University, his parents intended him for the ministry, but he chose literature as a profession instead. In 1823-4 his first considerable work, a *Life of Schiller*, was published serially in the *London Magazine* and was very highly praised. In 1826 Carlyle married Jane Baillie Welsh, a lineal descendent of John Knox, and during the same year appeared his *Specimens of German Romance*. From 1828 to 1834 he resided at Craigenputtoch, a small estate in Dumfriesshire, belonging to his wife—the "loneliest nook in Britain." One of his most beautiful, eloquent and solid essays, written there, was that on Burns. Also at Craigenputtoch was written *Sartor Resartus* ("The Tailor Done Over") in 1833. During the following year the Carlyles removed to London, taking a house in Cheyne Row, Chelsea. In 1837 appeared *The French Revolution*, universally held to be a prose epic. His *Heroes, and Hero-Worship, and the Heroic in History* was published in 1841, followed by what many consider his masterpiece, *Oliver Cromwell's Letters and Speeches, With Elucidations and a Connecting Narrative*. The sudden death of his wife, in 1866, overwhelmed Carlyle with grief. His life became more and more secluded. His work was now done, though he lived fifteen years longer.

❖ ❖ ❖

Earnestness of purpose and a passion for thoroughness were dominent traits of Thomas Carlyle. The greatest crime a man could commit, in his estimation, was to be false to himself. "Go to perdition if thou wilt," Hubbard quotes Carlyle as exclaiming, "but not with a lie in thy mouth—by the Eternal Maker, no!" In other words, any success worthy of the name must be won by honest and straightforward methods.

MARY W. SHELLEY

Born 1797—Died 1851 Volume II—Page 285

A GREAT POET'S INSPIRATION

"*It was Mary Wollstonecraft Godwin (Shelley) who awoke in Shelley such a burst of song that men yet listen to its cadence. It was she who gave his soul wings.*"—Hubbard.

❖

MARY WOLLSTONECRAFT SHELLEY, daughter of William Godwin and Mary Wollstonecraft, and wife of the poet Percy Bysshe Shelley, was born in London, and was buried at Bournemouth, England. Her life from 1814 to 1822 was bound up with that of Shelley, whom she married December 30, 1816. Their marriage occurred soon after the suicide of Shelley's first wife, Harriet Westbrook, with whom he had been estranged for some time. In that year Mary Shelley began writing her memorable novel, *Frankenstein*. It had its origin in a proposal of Lord Byron's that Mary and Shelley, Polidori (Byron's young physician), and Byron himself should write each a ghost story. *Frankenstein*, conceived in imitation of the old German stories of the supernatural, was published in 1818. Her second tale, *Valperga*, (1823) is a historical romance of mediæval Italy. Meanwhile the Shelleys were living in Italy, and there at Florence, in 1819, was borne Percy Florence Shelley, who was to inherit the Shelley title and estate. In July, 1821, Shelley and a male companion were drowned and their bodies were found upon the shore near Via Reggio. In 1823 Mary returned to England with her son. Her father-in-law, in granting her an allowance, insisted upon the suppression of a volume of Shelley's *Posthumous Poems*, edited by her. In *Lodore* (1835) she thinly disguised the story of Shelley's alienation from his first wife. Her last novel, *Falkner*, appeared in 1837.

❖ ❖ ❖

Next to doing a great work oneself, the utmost satisfaction may be gotten by helping some one else to succeed in a great undertaking. Such was the distinction of Mary Shelley.

HONORE DE BALZAC

Born 1799—Died 1850 **Volume XIII—Page 277**

THE GREATEST NOVELIST OF FRANCE

"*The leading traits in the life of Balzac were his ability to abandon himself to the task in hand, his infinite good-nature, his capacity for frolic and fun, and his passion to be famous and to be loved. . . .*"—Hubbard.

❖

HONORE DE BALZAC was born at Tours, France, the first of four children of well-to-do middle-class parents. As a boy he showed no cleverness in his studies. Nevertheless he had very early what his sympathetic sister Laura calls "the intuition of renown." A family misfortune was to him providential, for it took him at nineteen to Paris and acquaintances who stimulated his literary activity. He studied law, but refused to practice, and in spite of public and domestic discouragements he devoted himself to literature, doubting his power at times, but never his vocation. It took him ten years (1819-29) to fit himself to write *The Chouans*, one of the first and best of French historical novels. What follows it, good or bad, was admitted by Balzac to a place in his works, the greater portion of which consists of the novels grouped under the title of *The Human Comedy*. The next six years were years of marvelous fertility, sustained excellence and progressing power, fostered by intercourse with Hugo, Vigny, Lamartine and George Sand. Then he fell under the spell of a rich Polish lady, Madame Hanska, and for five years turned out successive masterpieces, notably *Eugénie Grandet*, his great study of avarice, and *Père Goriot*, thought by many to be his best novel. After 1847 he became absorbed in plans for marriage with Madame Hanska, who had become a widow, and was hindered from work by illness and by visits to the Polish estates of his betrothed. They were married a few months before his death.

❖ ❖ ❖

Early in life Balzac decided that there was one thing he desired to do above all else—to write fiction. He sacrificed everything to that end. Hubbard brings out the value, the necessity, of concentration and singleness of purpose in accomplishing any life work.

HARRIET MARTINEAU

Born 1802—Died 1876 Volume II—Page 69

A GREAT WOMAN PUBLICIST

"*Harriet Martineau was essentially an agitator. She entered into life in its fullest sense, and no phase of existence escaped her keen and penetrating investigation. . . . She was widely read, beloved, respected, feared and well hated.*"—Hubbard.

❖

HARRIET MARTINEAU was born at Norwich, England, where her father was a manufacturer. Her first appearance in print, in 1821, was an article in a religious journal. Intermittently she wrote *Devotional Exercises*, and short stories about machinery and wages. In 1829 the failure of a business enterprise in which the family fortunes were invested obliged her to earn her living. In the face of many discouragements, she wrote and published, in 1832, her *Illustrations of Political Economy*, which at once proved a popular success and made the author financially independent. She removed to London presently, the better to carry on her work. In 1834 she visited America, as a result of which she wrote *Society in America*, and a novel, *Deerbrook*, in 1839. After a winter in Venice, she settled at Tynemouth, England, where she remained, a complete invalid, till 1844. During her illness she wrote several volumes of juvenile tales. She recovered through mesmerism, it is said, and took upon a residence in the Lake Country, where she built herself a house at Ambleside. Her industry as a writer of fiction, essays and reviews was unflagging, and few literary-women have in their time enjoyed equal celebrity. Brought up in the Unitarian faith, Miss Martineau became an Agnostic, but her sympathy, kindness, mental integrity and impartiality of judgment won her international esteem and affection.

❖ ◆ ❖

Harriet Martineau exemplifies the woman or man whose dormant qualities and abilities are developed by adversity. Until a business failure wiped out her fortune and compelled her to work for a livelihood, this popular English authoress did not take literature seriously.

VICTOR HUGO

Born 1802—Died 1885 Volume I—Page 185

A GREAT FRENCH ROMANTICIST

"Men like Victor Hugo can be killed or they may be banished, but they cannot be bought; neither can they be intimidated into silence. . . ."—Hubbard.

❖

VICTOR MARIE HUGO, poet, dramatist, novelist, essayist and politician, was born at Besançon, France. For nearly two-thirds of the nineteenth century he was the recognized leader in French literature. In 1819 he started a fortnightly literary journal, the failure of which, with the withdrawal of an allowance from his father, reduced him to the condition of the character Marius in his great novel *Les Miserables*. The success of a volume of poetry and an improved financial prospect encouraged Hugo to take a wife at twenty, and it was a happy choice. The next few years were occupied with a romantic novel, *Hans of Iceland*, and other work preliminary to his plays *Cromwell* and *Marion Delorme*, the latter of which was barred from the stage until 1831. In 1829 Hugo published *Les Orientales*, a collection of poems containing some of the most striking pieces of metrical art in the world. They were followed by the triumph of his play, *Hernani*, and of Romanticism on the French stage (1830). His growing powers as a dramatist came to maturity in *Ruy Blas*, 1838, and *Les Burgraves*, 1843. Meanwhile he had published the novel, *The Hunchback of Notre Dame*, in 1831. Subsequently he threw himself into politics and became a revolutionary member of the Constituent Assembly of 1848. His political activities led to his exile from France and his residence on the isle of Guernsey, until the collapse of the Second Empire brought him back to France in 1870. Dying at 83, the body of Victor Hugo lay in state beneath the Arch of Triumph in Paris. His funeral was a pageant.

❖ ❖ ❖

Hugo made himself a supreme stylist. He developed an original, individual way of expressing himself. Time-worn formulas were not for him to follow. He put his own ideas into practise.

WILLIAM M. THACKERAY

Born 1811—Died 1863 Volume I—Page 229

A GREAT AUTHOR WITH NO ILLUSIONS

"In the realm of English letters, Thackeray is prince of humorists. He could see right through a brick wall, and never mistook a hawk for a hernshaw. He had a just estimate of values, and the temperament that can laugh at all trivial misfits."—Hubbard.

❖

WILLIAM MAKEPEACE THACKERAY was born at Calcutta, India, where his father was in the service of the East India Company. At the age of six the boy was sent to England, his father having meantime died, and placed in care of an aunt; but in 1821 his mother returned with her second husband and settled in Devonshire. The boy idolized her; and his stepfather, it is asserted, was the original of Colonel Newcome. Thackeray spent a year at Cambridge as a member of Trinity College and of the brilliant student group of which Tennyson was another ornament. After this he traveled abroad, staying some time at Weimar, where he met Goethe. Returning to London he studied law for a while at the Middle Temple, which furnished some of the material for *Pendennis.* On coming of age, he inherited a fortune of $100,000, but most of it was lost by the failure of an Indian bank, and he had to depend on his own exertions for a living. In 1833 he became editor and proprietor of the *National Standard,* which survived about a year. Thackeray then studied art in Paris. He sought to illustrate the *Pickwick Papers* for Dickens, but his services were declined. It was after his marriage, in 1836, to Isabella, daughter of Colonel Shawe of the Indian army, that Thackeray began to take authorship seriously, resulting in his great novels, *Vanity Fair, Pendennis, Henry Esmond, The Virginians.* In 1860 he became the first editor of the *Cornhill Magazine,* for which he wrote his last novels and the *Roundabout Papers.* The day before Christmas in 1863, Thackeray was found dead in his bed.

❖ ❖ ❖

Thackeray had the capacity of seeing himself as others saw him, and of laughing at himself along with others. To know oneself is to have a foot planted firmly on the ladder that leads upward.

WENDELL PHILLIPS

Born 1811—Died 1884 Volume VII—Page 385

AMERICAN ORATOR AND REFORMER

"When what you have done in the past looks large to you, you have not done much today. His hopes were so high that there crept into his life a tinge of disappointment—just a touch of sadness because he was unable to do more."—Hubbard.

❖

WENDELL PHILLIPS was born at Boston and was educated at Harvard and the Cambridge Law School. He became an Abolitionist at a time when the Constitutional right of an American citizen to own slaves was challenged by few, even in New England. He came at once into prominence by his Faneuil Hall speech of 1837 when, at the instance of Dr. William E. Channing, a public assembly had convened to protest against the murder of the Rev. E. P. Lovejoy, an Abolitionist, at Alton, Illinois. The purpose of the Faneuil Hall meeting was threatened with defeat, as Hubbard recounts, by the Attorney-General of Massachusetts, who commanded the Alton rioters, and affirmed that Lovejoy "died as the fool dieth." To this Phillips made a brilliant and crushing reply, the eloquence of which he never surpassed, and which has been ranked with Patrick Henry's oration at Williamsburg and Lincoln's Gettysburg address. From that time on Phillips was an Anti-Slavery leader, preëminently the orator of the movement. In 1840 he was the representative of the Massachusetts Abolitionists at the London World's Anti-Slavery Convention. Differences arose between himself and William Lloyd Garrison, who had converted him to the Abolition cause, over the reëlection of Lincoln in 1864. Phillips was dissatisfied with the Lincoln policy of conciliation. In 1865 Phillips advocated and Garrison opposed the continuance of the Anti-Slavery Society. It was continued, with Phillips replacing Garrison as president, until the passage of the Fifteenth Amendment in 1870.

❖ ❖ ❖

Wendell Phillips is the type of man who voluntarily foregoes popularity and the rewards of conventional success in order to champion a principle inimical to his interests, but which he considers right.

CHARLES DICKENS

Born 1812—Died 1870 Volume I—Page 247

A GREAT SELF-MADE NOVELIST

"Dickens received his education at the University of Hard Knocks. . . . Yet he became the most popular author the world has ever known, and up to the present time no writer of books has approached him in point of number of readers and of financial returns."—Hubbard.

❖

CHARLES DICKENS, the novelist, was born at Landport, then a suburb of Portsmouth, England. His father, who held a post in the navy pay office, was then stationed at Portsmouth, but when Charles was about five years old the family moved to London. The boy early developed a fondness for reading in the British Museum, and learned shorthand. He became a court and Parliamentary reporter, and in 1836 published a collection of essays and tales entitled *Sketches by Boz*. Encouraged by their success, he wrote the *Pickwick Papers*, first published serially 1836-7. Their popularity was unprecedented and the book marked an era in English literature. It was followed by *Oliver Twist*, 1837-9, and *Nicholas Nickleby*, 1838-9, *The Old Curiosity Shop*, 1840, and other works with clocklike regularity. After a visit to the United States, Dickens published in 1842 his *American Notes*, and in 1844 *Martin Chuzzlewit*. After this masterpiece his animal spirits were less exuberant; while, on the other hand, satire and pathos increased, as evidenced by *David Copperfield*, which Dickens preferred to all his other novels. In 1850 he started a weekly periodical, *Household Words*, afterwards merged in *All the Year Round*. In 1867 he again visited America, meeting with a brilliant reception. Dickens died while at work on *The Mystery of Edwin Drood*, and was buried in Westminster Abbey.

❖ ❖ ❖

It was his untiring industry, coupled with his self-developed genius, that enabled Dickens to turn out a novel a year for forty years, besides a dozen plays and other work. Dickens early learned that in order to keep up the standard and volume of his output he must labor methodically, not by fits and starts. From the Little Journey to this great English novelist we learn the value of "keeping forever at it."

HENRY WARD BEECHER

Born 1813—Died 1887 Volume VII—Page 345

GREATEST PULPIT ORATOR OF HIS TIME

"The influence of Henry Ward Beecher upon his time was marked. As a single drop of aniline in a barrel of water will tint the whole mass, so has the entire American mind been colored through the existence of this one glowing personality."—Hubbard.

❖

HENRY WARD BEECHER, son of the eminent theologian, Lyman Beecher, was born at Litchfield, Connecticut. His forensic talents were first manifested at the age of eleven in a debate with an older schoolmate over Paine's *Age of Reason*, young Beecher winning an orthodox victory. He graduated from Amherst College in 1834, studied theology under his father at Lane Seminary, and held pastorates at Lawrenceburg and Indianapolis, Indiana, from 1837 to 1847. In the latter year he was called to take charge of Plymouth Church, a new Congregational organization in Brooklyn, New York, which became noted for its bold advocacy of unpopular reforms, such as abolition and temperance. His congregation became one of the largest in America, and he addressed a greater audience through the public prints. His disregard of the conventional methods of preparing sermons, making few or no notes; and the physical strength that enabled him to deliver several discourses daily was scarcely less extraordinary than the eloquence, dramatic power, pathos and wit that characterized them. Addressing vast audiences in England on the purposes and issues of our Civil War, in 1863, he materially changed English public opinion. In 1874 he was sued for alienating the affections of a friend's (Theodore Tilton) wife, and the jury disagreed. Beecher strongly advocated free trade and woman suffrage.

❖ ❖ ❖

Henry Ward Beecher was a natural, full-blooded, give-and-take man, who happened to be eloquent. His great success lay in his ability to share the thoughts and feelings of the average individual—and to give them expression.

CHARLOTTE BRONTË

Born 1816—Died 1855 Volume II—Page 95

A GREAT WOMAN NOVELIST

"Charlotte Brontë wrote three great books. From the lonely, bleak parsonage on that stony hillside she sent forth her swaying filament of thought. She lived to know that she had won. Money came to her, all she needed, honors, friends and lavish praise."—Hubbard.

❖

CHARLOTTE BRONTË was born at Thornton, in the West Riding of Yorkshire, England. Her father was a clergyman of Irish descent (the name was originally Prunty). When Charlotte was eight years old she was sent with three of her sisters to a school between Leeds and Kendal, which she darkly pictured twenty-five years later in the pages of *Jane Eyre*. In 1831 Charlotte was sent to a school at Roehead, England, where her remarkable talents were recognized and where she formed several lifelong friendships. Subsequently she taught in the school. With a view to qualifying themselves for teaching, Charlotte and her sister, Emily, went to Brussels in 1842 and remained abroad two years. Returning home they found their father threatened with blindness and their only brother becoming an inebriate. Hoping to bolster the family fortunes, the sisters—Charlotte, Emily and Anne—turned their thoughts to literature. Their volume of poems was published in 1846 under the names of Currer, Ellis and Acton Bell; but it fell flat. Charlotte's next venture was a prose tale, *The Professor*, and while it was seeking a publisher, *Jane Eyre* was making progress. It appeared in 1847, and took the public by storm. Her next novel, *Shirley*, was published in 1849; and *Villette*, written under depressing circumstances, came out in 1853. Soon after Charlotte married her father's curate, the Rev. A. Nicholls, who had long known and loved her.

❖ ❖ ❖

Life dealt harshly with Charlotte Brontë, but she had the faculty of turning her trials and tribulations to marvellous account in fiction. The Little Journey to this great English woman novelist shows that no matter how great a misfortune one may experience, it can be made a source of strength and a starting point to future victory.

GEORGE ELIOT

Born 1819—Died 1880 Volume I—Page 49

FOREMOST ENGLISH WOMAN NOVELIST

"No woman has ever shown us power equal to that of George Eliot, in the subtle clairvoyance which divines the inmost play of passions, the experience that shows human capacity for contradiction, and the indulgence that is merciful because it understands."—Hubbard.

❖

GEORGE ELIOT is the pseudonym of Mary Ann Evans, who was born in Warwickshire, England. Her family are admittedly the prototypes of the Dodsons in *The Mill on the Floss;* there is much of her brother Isaac in the Tom Tulliver of the same novel; and critics have traced a resemblance between her father and Caleb Garth in *Middlemarch*, and have identified her mother with the inimitable Mrs. Poyser in *Adam Bede.* After attending the local schools of Nuneaton, she spent three years at a school in Coventry. The family moved to Coventry when George Eliot was twenty-one. As the result of a book review submitted to the *Westminster Review* she became assistant editor of that publication in 1850 and met many leading literary lights of the day. It was through Herbert Spencer that she met George Henry Lewes, with whom she lived for many years. A legal marriage was impossible, since Lewes had a wife living and was unable to get a divorce. It was through his influence and encouragement that George Eliot developed into a great novelist. Her first novel, *The Sad Fortunes of the Rev. Amos Barton* (1857), was followed by *Mr. Gilfil's Love Story* and *Janet's Repentance*, afterwards combined as *Scenes of Clerical Life.* It was applauded by Thackeray as the work of a man. Successively came from her pen *Adam Bede, The Mill on the Floss, Silas Marner, Romola, Felix Holt, The Spanish Gypsy, Middlemarch* and *Daniel Deronda.* In 1878 Lewes died, and two years later she married John Walter Cross. She died during the year of her marriage.

❖ ❖ ❖

That there is no essential difference between the mental power of men and women, given equal opportunities and encouragement, is shown in the Little Journey to George Eliot.

JOHN RUSKIN

Born 1819—Died 1900 Volume I—Page 87

A GREAT CRITIC

"*John Ruskin brings to bear an energy on every subject he touches that is sure to make the sparks of thought fly. His independent and fearless attitude awakens from slumber a deal of dozing intellect, and out of this strife of opinion comes truth.*"—Hubbard.

❖

JOHN RUSKIN was born in London, the son of a Scotch wine merchant, who amassed a fortune of £200,000. First educated by private tutors, he entered Christ Church, Oxford, in 1837, graduating in 1842. In the following year was published the first volume of his *Modern Painters*, the primary design of which was to prove the superiority of modern landscape painters, especially Turner, to the old masters. Being revolutionary in spirit and aim, the work naturally excited the hostility of conservatives. The first artists to accept Ruskin were the members of the Pre-Raphaelite Brotherhood, headed by Rossetti. Memorable is his defense of them against popular ridicule in his essay entitled *Pre-Raphaelitism* (1851). Ruskin published *The Seven Lamps of Architecture* (1849) and *The Stones of Venice* (1851-3), embodying a loftier conception of the significance of architecture. Other works followed, including a book of poems. A beautiful fairy tale *The King of the Golden River* and *Notes on the Construction of Sheepfolds* (1851), in which he brought forward a plan for Church unity in England. In 1865-6 appeared *Sesame and Lilies, Ethics of the Dust* and *The Crown of Wild Olive.* Ruskin was in great demand as a lecturer, and long occupied the chair of art at Oxford. He depleted his fortune in philanthropic works, but derived a large income from royalties on his books. Disposing of his home at Denmark Hill, near London, in 1871 Ruskin bought Brantwood, an estate on Coniston Lake, where he passed his last years and died.

❖ ❖ ❖

Ruskin is a notable example of the man who is born to riches, and yet devotes his life to useful work other than is concerned with money-making. Even to those of us who are not economically independent, the Little Journey to Ruskin is a reminder that means and leisure are necessary to certain work and that in employing them as he did, the great English art critic earned the applause of the world.

STARR KING

Born 1824—Died 1864 Volume VII—Page 309

A MARTYR TO ORATORY

"*Starr King, 'whose matchless oratory saved California to the Union,' gave his life to the Cause. He as much died for the Union as though he had fallen stricken by flying lead upon the field. In answer to warning friends he said: 'I have only one life to live and now is my time to spend it.'* "—Hubbard.

❖

THOMAS STARR KING was born in New York City. He studied theology while employed first as a retail store clerk and then as a school teacher in Massachusetts, and in 1846-8 was pastor of the Universalist Church at Charlestown, Mass. In 1848-60 he was pastor of the Hollis Street Unitarian Church of Boston, and during this period gained great popularity as a lyceum lecturer in the Northern States. He became pastor of the First Unitarian Society of San Francisco in 1860; was among the first to call attention to the wonders of the Yosemite Valley; and when, in the Presidential campaign of 1860, the idea of establishing California as an independent republic was discussed, he denounced the project from the lecture platform and kept the State for the Union. During the Civil War he exercised a powerful influence in favor of the Federal Government, and was active in obtaining in California large and necessary funds for the Sanitary Commission. He died, virtually from overwork, in San Francisco. One of the peaks of the White Mountains, which he explored during his New England residence and which first became generally known through his writings, has been named Starr King in his honor.

❖ ❖ ❖

To Starr King a Little Journey is made as an eminent pulpit-and-platform orator who greatly benefitted himself in mid-career by changing his environment completely. Frequently we think we have reached the final goal, when, as a matter of fact, we are only on the way to it.

FERDINAND LASSALLE

Born 1825—Died 1864 Volume XIII—Page 359

FOUNDER OF GERMAN SOCIAL-DEMOCRACY

"*A wise man has said that there is a difference between fact and truth. . . . The truth as to the love-story of Ferdinand Lassalle and Helene von Donniges can only be told by adhering strictly to the facts. Facts are not only stubborn things, but often very inconvenient.*"—Hubbard.

❖

FERDINAND LASSALLE, regarded as the originator of the social-democratic movement in Germany, was born at Breslau. Like Karl Marx, founder of international socialism, he was of Jewish extraction. He early displayed a distaste for trade, attended the universities of Breslau and Berlin, and by his extraordinary brilliancy attracted the attention of Alexander von Humboldt and other leaders of German thought. Lassalle took part in the revolution of 1848 and was imprisoned for six months in Düsseldorf. In 1861 he published *Das System der erworbenen Rechte*, pronounced by Savigny, founder of the modern school of jurisprudence, the ablest legal work written since the sixteenth century. A year later he came out as the champion of the working classes, and published several pamphlets which had a large surreptitious circulation. He could see no satisfactory prospect for the working classes under the wage system, but proposed to found coöperative associations for production, employing public credit to secure capital. In the summer of 1864 Lassalle met and wooed Helene von Donniges in Switzerland. Her parents frowned upon him as a prospective son-in-law and insisted that she marry a Wallachian nobleman. In his rage and mortification Lassalle challenged her father and fiancé to a duel. The challenge was accepted by the latter, who mortally wounded Lassalle.

❖ ❖ ❖

The Little Journey to Lassalle points out the danger of mixing sentiment and business, or rather of allowing distracting influences to interfere with one's life work. Midway in his gigantic task of revolutionizing the German social order, Lassalle indulged in a disastrous romance.

DANTE GABRIEL ROSSETTI

Born 1828—Died 1882 Volume XIII—Page 247

A GREAT POET AND PAINTER

"A year after the death of his wife Rossetti painted the wonderful Beata Beatrix. . . . And in all the pictures thereafter painted by him, you perceive that while he had various models, in them all he traced resemblances to this first, last and only passion of his life."—Hubbard.

❖

DANTE GABRIEL ROSSETTI, head of what is known as the Pre-Raphaelite Brotherhood, was born in London of Italian parentage. At twenty he became a pupil of the artist Ford Madox Brown, whose influence had much to do with his development. With Holman Hunt, Millais and others, Rossetti worked toward the revival of the detailed elaboration and mystical interpretation that characterized Pre-Raphaelite art. In 1860 he married Elizabeth Eleanor Siddal, whose peculiar type of beauty is immortalized in many of his pictures. She died two years later, and Rossetti never recovered from the shock. In addition to this grief he was much troubled by a bitter attack made in 1871 upon the morality of his poems, in an anonymous article entitled *The Fleshly School of Poetry.* The charge was vigorously rebutted by Swinburne, and by Rossetti himself under the title *The Stealthy School of Criticism.* His mental depression brought on, by 1868, chronic insomnia, for which he sought to find relief in chloral. He fell a victim to the drug, and became subject to a tragic gloom relieved only by the creative play of his mind, which continued almost to the last to produce pictures and poems of singular beauty. It is hard to say whether Rossetti deserves a more lasting place in the history of poetry or in that of painting. Among his pictures *Dante's Dream* perhaps shows the painter at his zenith. Of his poems, *The Blessed Damosel,* written at twenty, is the best known, if not the greatest. This, with his other poems in manuscript, was buried with his wife, and so remained for seven years. The manuscripts were exhumed and published in 1870.

❖ ❖ ❖

Rossetti illustrates the possibility of a man being a supreme master of two great accomplishments at the same time. He was equally proficient as a poet and as a painter. The Little Journey brings out the advantage one can derive by having more than one important interest in life.

CHARLES BRADLAUGH

Born 1833—Died 1891 Volume IX—Page 243

A GREAT RADICAL ORATOR

"Charles Bradlaugh performed for England the same service that Robert Ingersoll did for America. . . . His interest along similar lines cost him the foremost position at the English bar. The man had presence, persistence, courage, and that rapid, ready intellect which commands respect with judge, jury and opposition."—Hubbard.

❖

CHARLES BRADLAUGH was a native of London, England. His early education was meager, and at seventeen he enlisted in the army. Obtaining his discharge in 1853, he became clerk to a London solicitor, and soon was noted as an agitator, free thought lecturer and as a pamphleteer. He published the *National Reformer*. In 1873 he visited the United States, lecturing in the larger cities. In 1876, with Mrs. Annie Besant, he was sentenced to six months in prison and £200 fine for republishing the Malthusian *Fruits of Philosophy*, but the conviction was quashed on appeal. Elected to Parliament from Northampton in 1880, he pleaded that as an atheist he had the right to affirm, but when this request was denied, expressed his willingness to take the oath. This the House of Commons decided he was disqualified from doing; he was ordered to leave, and on his refusal was placed in custody. His seat was declared vacant, but his constituency returned him in 1881. Again he was denied the privilege of taking the oath, and was forcibly ejected from the House. Similar scenes occurred in 1882-3. Two years later he was again returned for Northampton, and was permitted to take the oath. Shortly before his death, Parliament expunged from its records the resolution forbidding him to take the oaths.

❖ ❖ ❖

Hubbard devotes a Little Journey to Charles Bradlaugh as a reformer who throve on opposition. Unless something had to be fought for, it was not worth possessing, in his estimation. In other words, the prizes of life are only to be won by constant exertion and earnest effort.

ROBERT INGERSOLL

Born 1833—Died 1899 Volume VII—Page 233

EMINENT AMERICAN ORATOR

"*Every change to him meant progress. Success is a question of temperament—it is all a matter of the red corpuscle. Ingersoll was a success; happy, exuberant, joying in life, reveling in existence.*"—Hubbard.

❖

ROBERT GREEN INGERSOLL was born at Dresden, New York, the youngest of five children of a Congregational minister of liberal views. The family removed to Illinois in 1845, and there Robert studied law and was admitted to the bar. He established a practice at Peoria and became prominent in politics. In 1862 he took part in the Civil War as colonel of the Eleventh Illinois Cavalry, and was taken prisoner, but exchanged. He returned to civil life, and was appointed Attorney General of Illinois in 1868. In 1876, at the Republican National Convention, his "plumed knight" speech in favor of the candidacy of James G. Blaine won him a national reputation, and from then on he was recognized as a foremost orator of the country. He entered the lecture field and developed the views of a pronounced opponent to Christianity. Adopting religious topics as his subjects, he attacked the Bible, the personal nature of the Deity, and the existence of a hell, with effective eloquence. His theological views coincided with those of Thomas Paine. Colonel Ingersoll was president of several railroad companies and counsel for large corporations. His death occurred suddenly at Dobbs Ferry, New York.

❖ ❖ ❖

Ingersoll is another example of the man who thrives on opposition. Success of a kind is comparatively easy, if one encounters nothing but support and encouragement. It is another matter to make headway against hostile forces such as were arrayed against Ingersoll.

ROBERT LOUIS STEVENSON

Born 1850—Died 1894 Volume XIII—Page 11

A SCOTCH ROMANCER

"*As a writer of exquisite humor, as opposed to English wit, Robert Louis Stevenson stands supreme. To him life was altogether too important a matter to be taken seriously. . . . The gentle spirit of Stevenson lives again in the common heart of the world in lives made better.*"—Hubbard.

❖

ROBERT LOUIS STEVENSON was born in Edinburgh, the only son of a distinguished lighthouse engineer. He entered Edinburgh University in 1867, with the intention of becoming an engineer himself. This intention was soon altered, however, in favor of his becoming a barrister. He was admitted to the bar in 1875, but never practised. An early and strong bent for literature was encouraged by established men of letters whom he met in London, and while still in his twenties he wrote *An Inland Voyage* and *Travels With a Donkey*, sketches which reveal an exquisite literary art. At that time he also wrote some of his best essays, afterward collected under the titles of *Virginibus Puerisque* (1881) and *Familiar Studies of Men and Books* (1882), besides the fantastic *New Arabian Nights*. In 1876 he had met, in an art colony near Paris, Mrs. Osbourne, an American lady, who afterwards became his wife. In 1879 he followed her to America and spent two years in California, writing desultorily and very much handicapped by poor health and a frail physique. Success first came to him with the publication in 1883 of *Treasure Island*, a tale of adventure. *Dr. Jekyll and Mr. Hyde* (1886) further enhanced his reputation. It was followed by *Kidnapped*, which, with its sequel, *David Balfour* (1893), and *The Master of Ballantrae* (1889) present vivid pictures of the Scottish life of the past. The Stevensons located on a Samoan island in the South Seas in 1888, and there Robert Louis did all his subsequent work. His death at forty-four was caused by a lesion of the brain. He was buried on the peak of Mount Vaea, above Vailima, his Samoan home.

❖ ❖ ❖

That poor health and a weak body are not insuperable handicaps to the doing of great work is shown in the Little Journey to Robert Louis Stevenson. Destined to die at a comparatively early age, he was never discouraged. On the contrary, his industry in the brief time given him to do his work was astonishing.

BOOK FOUR

❖

SCIENCE AND INVENTION

LEONARDO

Born 1452—Died 1519 Volume VI—Page 39

MANY-SIDED MASTER OF THE RENAISSANCE

"*Leonardo studied Nature at first hand—he took nothing for granted—Nature was his one book. He was a geologist, a botanist, an engineer. He was indeed the endless experimenter—his was in very truth the Experimental Life. . . . To try many things means power: to finish a few is immortality.*"—Hubbard.

❖

LEONARDO DA VINCI was born at Vinci, a Tuscan mountain town near Empoli, and was the natural son of Ser Piero da Vinci, a Florentine notary. He was well educated, and before taking up painting he began the studies in mechanics which went hand in hand with his artistic activity throughout life. Going to Milan about 1483 he entered the service of its ruler as chief military engineer, constructor of the Martesana Canal and director of pageants. He also was active as an architect, being employed upon the Cathedral of Milan, and he probably designed other public buildings. He found time to prosecute his studies in anatomy, especially of animals, and to become a proficient mathematician. Toward the close of the fifteenth century Leonardo executed his masterpiece of painting, *The Last Supper*. Most of his other pictures painted during this period have been lost. Of his surviving portraits, the best-known is the *Mona Lisa* in the Louvre, Paris, completed about 1504, and *La belle Ferronnière*. A portrait of him, by himself, is in the Royal Library, Turin. As a man of science, aside from being a master painter and musician, Leonardo towered above all contemporaries, and had his views been known and generally published, they must have revolutionized the science of his day.

❖ ❖ ❖

Leonardo da Vinci is an example of the man who is equally proficient in any line of work he undertakes. However, he made it a point to undertake only one thing at a time. The Little Journey to Leonardo is a reminder that by systematizing one's work and avoiding confusion one can get astonishing results, as compared with any other method.

COPERNICUS

Born 1473—Died 1543 Volume XII—Page 87

FOUNDER OF MODERN ASTRONOMY

"*In astronomy Copernicus found a means of using his mighty mathematical genius for his own pleasure and amusement. . . . He knew what all other great astronomers had taught, and out of them all he had built a Science of Astronomy that he knew would stand secure.*"—Hubbard.

❖

NICHOLAS COPERNICUS (Latinized form of Koppernigk) was born at Thorn, a Prussian town on the Vistula, at that time in Poland. Graduating from the University of Cracow, in 1495 he went to Italy and spent some years in the study of law, astronomy and medicine, at Bologna and Padua. Proceeding to Rome he met Regiomontanus, then the most illustrious of astronomers. The year 1500 he spent in Rome, lecturing on mathematics and astronomy, and "observed an eclipse of the moon." Five years later he returned to his native country and became canon of the Cathedral of Frauenburg. There he passed the remaining thirty-eight years of his life. Copernicus divided his working day into three parts—one devoted to the duties of his office, another to giving medical advice gratuitously to the poor, and the third to study. Soon after his return to Prussia, he began, in 1507, to apply his fund of observations and mathematical knowledge to correcting the system of astronomy which then prevailed. The result was his *De Revolutionibus Orbium*, completed in 1530. Twelve years elapsed before he overcame the fear of drawing upon himself the wrath of the Church, and published the work. It was dedicated to Pope Paul III. Copernicus died a few hours after a first copy of it reached him.

❖ ❖ ❖

To those who are inclined to accept hearsay for fact and to jump too quickly to conclusions, the Little Journey to Copernicus is recommended. The father of modern astronomy would take nothing for granted. He furnishes an example of accuracy and thoroughness that can be followed by everyone with benefit.

GALILEO

Born 1564—Died 1642 Volume XII—Page 47

GREAT ASTRONOMER AND INVENTOR

"The year Sixteen Hundred Nine is forever fixed in history, through the fact that in that year Galileo invented the telescope. . . . He was getting to be more than a professor of mathematics—he was becoming a power in the world. The lever of his mighty mind was finding a fulcrum."—Hubbard.

❖

GALILEO GALILEI was born at Pisa, of a Florentine family more ancient than opulent. Attending the University of Pisa, he devoted himself to mathematics and physical science. At eighteen he made his first important discovery—the clock pendulum. Turning his attention to geometry, in his early twenties he invented the hydrostatic balance, by which the specific gravity of solid bodies might be accurately ascertained. In 1589 he was appointed to the chair of mathematics at his alma mater. Removing to Padua, in 1592, he accepted the invitation of the Venetian Senate to lecture on mathematics in the university there for a period of six years, eventually prolonged to eighteen years. Pupils flocked to hear him from all parts of Europe. In 1609 he offered his first complete telescope to the Doge of Venice, who tested it from the tower of Saint Mark. In the same year he constructed a microscope. In 1611, following his epoch-making astronomical researches, he visited Rome and was received with great distinction. Four years later he was charged with heresy for advocating the Copernican system, and was warned to desist. In 1632 he published his *Dialogue On the Two Chief Systems*, was tried by the Inquisition and sentenced to imprisonment. The sentence was commuted, and Galileo spent his declining years in Florence, where he was buried in the Cathedral of Santa Croce.

❖ ❖ ❖

Galileo discovered to his cost that to upset an established belief or notion —even though it be a false one—is to invite trouble for oneself. In the Little Journey devoted to the great astronomer-inventor, Hubbard dwells especially upon the risks that attend any innovation however much it may benefit mankind.

SIR ISAAC NEWTON

Born 1642—Died 1727 Volume XII—Page 11

DISCOVERER OF THE LAW OF GRAVITATION

"The verdict of humanity concerning Sir Isaac Newton has been summed up for us thus by Laplace: 'His work was pre-eminent above all other products of the human intellect.' "—Hubbard.

❖

ISAAC NEWTON was born at Woolsthorpe, near Grantham, Lincolnshire, and died at Kensington, England. He matriculated at Cambridge University in 1661, and graduated in 1665, the year in which the method of fluxions first occurred to him. He was made a fellow of Trinity College in 1667 and Lucasian professor in 1669. He became a fellow of the Royal Society in 1672. Newton's attention was probably drawn to the subject of gravitation as early as 1665. Kepler had established the laws of the planetary orbits, and from them Newton proved that the attraction of the sun upon the planets varies inversely as the squares of their distances. The success of his work really depended on the determination of the length of a degree on the earth's surface by Picard in 1671. The universal law of gravitation was completely elaborated by 1685, a year before Newton presented his *Principia* to the Royal Society. In 1689 he sat in Parliament for Cambridge University. When his friend Charles Montagu (afterward Earl of Halifax) was made Chancellor of the Exchequer, Newton was made Warden and subsequently Master of the Mint. The reformation of English coinage was largely his work. In 1699 he was elected foreign associate of the French Academy of Sciences. In 1703 he became president of the Royal Society, and held the office till his death.

❖ ❖ ❖

Newton is a most eminent example of the man who reasons things out for himself and never rests until he finds a certain answer to a given question. Seeing an apple fall to the ground, he queried why, and proceeded to discover the law of gravitation. Inquiring minds of the Newton order are behind all progress and prosperity.

LINNÆUS

Born 1707—Died 1778 Volume XII—Page 265

A GREAT SWEDISH BOTANIST

"Linnæus shifted the scientific center of gravity of all Europe to a town [Upsala, Sweden]. His life flowed forward like a great and mighty river—everything made way for him. Universities in many civilized countries honored themselves by giving him degrees."—Hubbard.

❖

CAROLUS LINNÆUS, originator of the modern scientific methods of naming plants and animals, was born at Rashult, Province of Smaland, Sweden. He was educated for the ministry, but early exhibited a fondness for botany, and in 1732 he was commissioned by the Academy of Sciences of Upsala to conduct a scientific exploration of Lapland. His botanical results were published five years later in his *Flora Lapponica*. Subsequently he made a scientific journey through Dalecarlia at the invitation of the Governor. In 1835 Linnæus visited Holland and published his *Systema Naturae*, which quickly went through twelve editions. During his residence of four years there he published four other works and attained an international reputation. In 1739, having obtained a degree as doctor of medicine, he was appointed Naval Physician and became president of the Academy at Stockholm. Two years later he occupied the chair of medicine at the University of Upsala and remained there thirty-seven years. His reputation became unique and world-wide. In 1761 he received the title of nobility. At the age of sixty his remarkable memory began to fail. From 1774 to the time of his death he suffered greatly as the result of apoplexy, having had no use of his right side for two years before he finally succumbed. He was buried in the cathedral at Upsala.

❖ ❖ ❖

In making the science of botany yield him unprecedented honors, Linnæus illustrates the fact that the world is ever ready to acclaim and reward any one who can do something even of least regarded value better than any one else. Until his time botany was a neglected science. The Little Journey makes plain the advisability of developing one's natural bent or talent, no matter what obstacles may be in the way.

WILLIAM HERSCHEL

Born 1738—Died 1822 Volume XII—Page 165

FOUNDER OF SIDEREAL SCIENCE

"One real secret of Herschel's influence seems to have been his fine enthusiasm. He worked with such vim, such animation, that he radiated light on every side. He set others to work, and his love for astronomy as a science created a demand for telescopes, which he himself had to supply."—Hubbard.

❖

SIR WILLIAM HERSCHEL was born at Hanover, Germany, the son of a musician. In 1757 he went to England, where he became a music teacher at Leeds and later at Bath. There he first turned his attention to astronomy. Wanting a telescope, and unable to afford a reflector, he made one for himself. His first astronomical discovery, in 1781, was of a new planet, which he at first mistook for a comet. As a result he was appointed private astronomer to King George III, with a salary of £200 a year. Thereafter he lived at Slough, near Windsor, where, aided by his sister, Caroline, he continued his researches. Herschel contributed sixty-nine papers to the Astronomical Society. He discovered Uranus (called by him Georgium Sidus), and the two satellites of Saturn, the rotation of whose ring he first detected, along with that of Venus. He extended our knowledge of the Milky Way and the constitution of nebulae, and, in fact, was the first to give the human mind any conception of the immensity of the universe. It was by means of his great 40-foot telescope, finished in 1789, he detected the sixth and seventh satellites of Saturn. Herschel left one son, Sir John, his only rival in the field of English astronomy. He was knighted by George III, and made a D. C. L. by the University of Oxford.

❖ ❖ ❖

That a hobby or side issue may become a great and profitable life work, is shown in the Little Journey to Herschel. His original profession was that of a music teacher, and he at first took up the study of astronomy as a diversion. Gradually the scientist supplanted the musician, with momentous results in the field of astronomy.

HUMBOLDT

Born 1769—Died 1859 Volume XII—Page 123

FIRST OF PHYSICAL GEOGRAPHERS

"Humboldt had imagination to see the thing first with his inward eye; he had the strength to endure physical discomfort, and finally he had money enough so he was free to follow his bent."—Hubbard.

❖

ALEXANDER VON HUMBOLDT was born in Berlin and his youth was spent in the old Castle of Tegel, near Potsdam. He first studied under private tutors and then at the Universities of Frankfort-on-the-Oder, Berlin and Göttingen. In 1791 he entered the Academy of Mining at Freiberg. His work there secured him the directorship of mines in Bayreuth and Anspach, where he resided for three years. In 1795 he was at Jena, in company with Goethe and Schiller. There he began to plan for the great journey to Spanish America with which his fame is most permanently associated. Subsequently in Paris he made the acquaintance of a young French botanist, Aimé Bonpland, who accompanied him to South America in 1799. They explored the upper waters of the Orinoco and established the connection between that river and the Amazon. The year 1801 was spent in Cuban explorations, the basin of the Magdalena River and in the Andes of Ecuador, the famous ascent of Chimborazo being accomplished in 1802. A year in Mexico was followed by a visit to the United States, en route to Paris, where, in 1807, Humboldt began publishing the results of the great *Voyage*. Between 1845 and 1858 appeared volume by volume his *Kosmos*, an encyclopaedic account and explanation of the physical universe.

❖ ❖ ❖

Alexander von Humboldt was "always a student, always an investigator, always a tireless worker." Here we have the type of individual who does not have to work for a living, but who finds no satisfaction in idleness. It is men of this character who contribute most generously to the progress of civilization.

CHARLES DARWIN

Born 1809—Died 1882. Volume XII—Page 199

GREATEST MODERN NATURALIST

"Charles Darwin was not only the greatest thinker of his time (with possibly one exception), but in his simplicity and earnestness, in his love for truth—his perfect willingness to abandon his opinion if he were found to be wrong—he proved himself the greatest man of his time."—Hubbard.

❖

CHARLES DARWIN was born the same day, February 12, 1809, that Abraham Lincoln was. He was the grandson of Erasmus Darwin, a distinguished physician and naturalist, and of Josiah Wedgwood, the famous manufacturer of pottery. Educated at Edinburgh and Cambridge, his parents originally intended him for the ministry, but hereditary tendencies toward natural history led him in another direction. Shortly after graduation he seized an opportunity to go around the world as naturalist in H. M. S. *Beagle*, commanded by Captain Fitz-Roy, R. N. This expedition spent most of the time between 1831 and 1836 in making surveys of southern South America, which afforded Darwin a great opportunity for making original observations. His studies on the fauna of the Galapagos Islands brought him to a conception of the famous Darwinian theory of evolution. His account of the expedition (1860) is entitled *Voyage of a Naturalist on H. M. S. Beagle.* Other important books followed, including his valuable *Monograph of the Cirripedia* (study of barnacles), and in 1859 appeared his great work on *The Origin of Species.* Largely through the able championship of Huxley, its idea soon gained widespread acceptance, though challenged in many quarters. It revolutionized the method of work and the aims of natural history. Before Darwin, comparative anatomy was the comparison of types; since then it has become the study of the effect of function and environment in molding the bodily form.

The great lesson that Darwin taught, as set forth in the Little Journey by Hubbard, is that the man who "keeps fit" is bound to get the big prizes in the struggle for existence. He calls it "the survival of the fittest," which simply means that the trained man wins, develops most completely, by taking the fullest advantage of his opportunities.

JOHN TYNDALL

Born 1820—Died 1893 Volume XII—Page 335

A GREAT ENGLISH PHYSICIST

"*Herbert Spencer avowed again and again that Tyndall was the greatest teacher he ever knew or heard of, inspiring the pupil to discover for himself, to do, to become, rather than imparting prosy facts of doubtful pith and moment.*"—Hubbard.

JOHN TYNDALL was born at Leighlin Bridge, County Carlow, Ireland. His first employment was in a subordinate grade of the Ordnance Survey, and later as a railroad engineer. He became a teacher of mathematics and surveying at Queenwood College, Hampshire, England, in 1847. His first communication to the Royal Society, in 1853, was on the *Transmission of Heat Through Organic Structures*, followed by one *On the Influence of Material Aggregation Upon the Manifestations of Force*, which inaugurated his reputation as a lecturer. A few months later he was appointed professor of natural history in the Royal Institution, becoming a colleague of Faraday, whom he succeeded as director in 1867. Tyndall spent much time in the Alps, where he combined mountain-climbing with scientific research, making numerous careful observations of the great Swiss glaciers. His discoveries in connection with radiant energy led to improved methods of sterilization. As scientific adviser to Trinity House (in charge of the lighthouse service) and the British Board of Trade, Tyndall carried on a number of experiments with direct practical ends. Aside from his written works, he achieved international repute as a lecturer and greatly contributed to the popularization of science. Few scientists have been able to present the principles and facts of physics to the general public so successfully as Tyndall.

If all the people on earth were Tyndalls there would be no rival political parties and no conflicting religions or church denominations. With small respect for conventions or traditions, a Tyndall would never be influenced by a sense of party loyalty to vote contrary to his conviction, or to bow to anything but truth.

JAMES OLIVER

Born 1823—Died 1908 Volume XI—Page 53

INVENTOR OF THE CHILLED PLOW

"Oliver, being a farmer, knew that there was not a good plow in the world. . . . He insisted that an approximately perfect plow could be made. He realized that a good plow should stay in the ground without wearing out the man at the handles."—Hubbard.

❖

JAMES OLIVER was born in Roxburyshire, Scotland, and died at South Bend, Indiana. He came to America in 1835 with his parents, who, after residing a year in Seneca County, New York, settled in Lagrange County, Indiana, and later moved to Mishawaka, Saint Joseph County. At that time (1836) Mishawaka, advantageously located on the Saint Joseph River, promised to become a metropolis such as Indianapolis is today. James had but one year of schooling, the death of his father in 1837 making it necessary for him to go to work. He learned the trade of an iron molder and then became a cooper, at which occupation he prospered to the extent of being able, in 1855, to buy a quarter interest in a foundry at South Bend, Indiana. Cast-iron plows constituted the principal output of the foundry. It was not long before Oliver realized that there was great room for improvement in plow construction, and after twelve years of experimenting he succeeded in perfecting what is known as the chilled plow. It involved three inventions, the third of which was the annealing process which strengthened and tempered the moldboard without detracting from its wearing and scouring qualities, making the chilled plow a complete success and its originator a multimillionaire.

In the Little Journey devoted to the inventor of the chilled plow Hubbard observes that James Oliver worked for one thing and got another. He sought to benefit his farming fellows by making a good plow. Having succeeded in that ambition, he automatically became a plow manufacturer of international repute and a benefactor of mankind.

ALFRED R. WALLACE

Born 1823—Died 1913 Volume XII—Page 367

A GREAT ENGLISH NATURALIST-PHILOSOPHER

"Wallace holds that it is better to plow than to pray, and that in fact, when rightly understood, good plowing is prayer. All useful effort is sacred, and nothing else is or ever can be. Wallace believes that the only fit preparation for the future lies in improving the present."—Hubbard.

❖

ALFRED RUSSEL WALLACE was born at Usk, Monmouthshire, England. Receiving a grammar school education, he was articled to a land surveyor and architect. He early developed a passion for entomology, and in 1848 sailed for a four-year sojourn in the Amazon Valley. It marked an epoch in scientific travel and resulted in *A Narrative of Travels on the Amazon and Rio Negro*, published in 1853. Another result was his work on *Palm Trees of the Amazon and Their Uses*. Of still greater importance to the progress of modern biological geography and philosophy was his eight years residence in the Malay Archipelago, which led him to formulate his theory of natural selection and write that scientific classic, *The Malay Archipelago, the Land of the Orang-Utan and the Bird of Paradise*. His natural selection theory was first outlined in a paper he sent to Charles Darwin. July 1, 1858, it was read before the Linnæan Society together with a statement of the practically identical theory which Darwin had been elaborating independently for years. What has come to be known as the Wallace Line marks the boundary between an Asiatic and an Australian fauna in the archipelago. Wallace stands by pure Darwinism, refusing to admit the additional elements, such as sexual selection, which Darwin adopted in his later works. Wallace was a voluminous writer on many subjects, including sociology and spiritualism.

That no spirit of rivalry existed between Wallace and Darwin, who simultaneously hit upon the doctrine of natural selection, is a point made in the Little Journey to the former. Both Wallace and Darwin were too big and busy to attempt to discredit each other in the eyes of the world. It is only small natures that are fearful of not getting credit due them for doing good work.

THOMAS H. HUXLEY

Born 1825—Died 1895 Volume XII—Page 305

A GREAT ENGLISH NATURALIST

"*The controlling impulse of Huxley's life was his absolute honesty. To pretend to believe a thing against which one's reason revolts, in order to better one's place in society, was to him the sum of all that was intellectually base.*"—Hubbard.

❖

THOMAS HENRY HUXLEY was born at Ealing, now a suburb of London. He studied in the Medical School of Charing Cross Hospital, and in 1845 was graduated as M. B. and medalist at the University of London. The following year he was appointed assistant surgeon on the *Rattlesnake* of the Royal Navy, commissioned to survey the region of the Great Barrier Reef, east and north of Australia. Huxley devoted himself to the study of marine life, and his discoveries stand at the basis of modern philosophical zoölogy, and of a true conception of the affinity of animals. In 1854 he occupied the chair of natural history and paleontology at the Royal School of Mines, and from thence on was the recipient of honors in one important post after another throughout his life. In 1871 he succeeded to the secretaryship of the Royal Society, of which he became president in 1883; in 1872 he was made lord rector of Aberdeen University; in 1881 he was professor of biology in the Royal College of Science, and in 1892 was Privy Councilor. Huxley came to America in 1876 and lectured to large audiences on the subject of Evolution, of which he was an ardent champion from the beginning. His own contributions to science were of the widest range and embraced every department of biology. Following a lingering illness he died at Eastbourne, England.

❖ ❖ ❖

Huxley, although a great scientist on his own account, is most widely known as a champion of the Darwinian theory of Evolution. It was his simple and honest belief in its truth that caused him to acclaim Darwinism, not through any design to share the limelight with Darwin. To Huxley a Little Journey is made as one who, instead of being jealous of a fellow-worker, generously endorsed him and thereby unconsciously benefitted himself and mankind.

HAECKEL

Born 1834—Died 1919 Volume XII—Page 237

GREATEST OF MODERN ZOOLOGISTS

"The Haeckel attitude of mind is essentially one of faith—Haeckel's hope for the race is sublime. . . . 'I and my Father are one'—the thought is old, but to prove it from the so-called material world through the study of biology has been the life-work of Ernst Haeckel."—Hubbard.

❖

ERNST HAECKEL was born at Potsdam, near Berlin, and died at Jena, Germany, where he had taught at the university for forty-six years. After taking his medical degree at Berlin, in 1857, and practising for a year, he abandoned medicine for zoölogy and studied marine life in Heligoland, Sicily and Naples. He joined the Jena faculty in 1862, and made numerous scientific journeys to the Canary Islands, to Norway, the Adriatic, the Red Sea, Corsica, Sardinia, Ceylon and Java. In 1866 appeared his *History of Creation*, a popular exposition of the doctrine of evolution, which has had the widest circulation and done more to popularize Darwinism in Germany than any other book. A corresponding work dealing specifically with the descent of man appeared in 1874, entitled *The Evolution of Man*. The frankly antitheological character of these writings drew upon Haeckel the anathemas of the Church. The manifesto of his monistic creed was published in 1899 under the title of *The Riddle of the Universe*. It has had an immense popularity among free-thinking people. Supplementing it was his *Miracles of Life* (1914). On his eightieth birthday Haeckel received a title of nobility. His thoughts on the World War were expressed in his last work, *Eternity*, published in 1916.

❖ ❖ ❖

In the Little Journey to Haeckel we are in contact with a man whose great career was determined by the chance reading of a book. Haeckel had intended to be a physician until Darwin's Origin of Species fell into his hands and caused him to become a zoölogist. His case serves as a reminder that one's whole course of life may be changed at any time by sudden contact with something or somebody of whose existence one has no forewarning.

John Fiske

Born 1842—Died 1901 Volume XII—Page 397

"Greatest American Scientist"

"John Fiske made the science of Darwin and Wallace palatable to orthodox theology, and it is to the earnest and eloquent words of Fiske that we owe it that Evolution is taught everywhere in the public schools and even in the sectarian colleges of America today."—Hubbard.

❖

JOHN FISKE, whose original name was Edmund Fiske Green, was born at Hartford, Conn. On the second marriage of his widowed mother he assumed the name of his maternal great-grandfather. He was graduated at Harvard College in 1863, and at the Harvard Law School in 1865, but never engaged in the practice of law seriously. In 1869 he began a distinguished career as a lecturer at Harvard, his general subject being *Philosophy in Its Evolutionary Aspect.* A year later he was made instructor of history, and in 1872 assistant librarian, a post which he held for five years. In 1884 he became professor of American History in Washington University, Saint Louis, and retained the chair for some years. His reputation was already international, for he had lectured on American history at University College, London, in 1879, and at the Royal Institution of Great Britain in 1880. During the earlier part of his career his interest was mainly in the study of evolution, and it was as a popularizer of its philosophy that he first became known nationally, through *Outlines of Cosmic Philosophy* (1874). His *American Political Ideas Viewed from the Standpoint of Universal History* was published in 1885, and with this began a period devoted to investigations in American history that constitute his most valuable contributions to American literature and to the molding of the national life.

❖ ❖ ❖

A Little Journey is devoted to John Fiske as a great recognizer, rather than discoverer, of scientific truth. As Hubbard observes, to recognize a great thing is next in importance to creating or discovering it. If you cannot originate and execute a work yourself, you can assist and encourage someone else to do so.

Thomas A. Edison

Born 1847 Volume I—Page 321

Greatest of American Inventors

"*You cannot look out of a window in any city in Europe or America without beholding the influence of his thought. . . . As Athens at her height was the Age of Pericles, so will our time be known as the Age of Edison.*"—Hubbard.

❖

THOMAS ALVA EDISON was born at Milan, Ohio. His family moved to Port Huron, Michigan, when he was seven years of age, but he obtained no schooling, and at the age of twelve became a railway newsboy. Later he was a telegraph operator. At Indianapolis, in 1864, he invented an automatic telegraph repeater, the first of his many inventions. Soon afterward he went to Boston and there invented a commercial stock indicator, which he sold for $40,000. This enabled him to establish a laboratory at Newark, N. J. Subsequently he has had laboratories at Menlo Park and at West Orange, N. J., giving employment to thousands of workmen in the service of probably the greatest inventor of modern times. More than 1,000 patents have been issued to him. Among his more important inventions are the phonograph, long-distance telephone, a system of duplex telegraphy (which he subsequently developed into quadruplex and sextuplex transmission), the carbon telephone transmitter, the megaphone, the incandescent electric lamp, the kinetoscope, a storage battery for street railway cars and automobiles. There is not an electrical instrument or process in use but bears the stamp of his genius. He made many war inventions for the United States Government, and has received honors too numerous to mention.

❖ ❖ ❖

In defining genius as "2 per cent. inspiration and 98 per cent. perspiration," Edison gives encouragement to those who regard themselves handicapped by lack of talent or natural advantages. The secret of success is seen in the Little Journey to the great American inventor to lie mainly in hard work intelligently directed.

BOOK FIVE

❖

PAINTING AND SCULPTURE

BELLINI

Born 1426—Died 1516 Volume VI—Page 249

FOUNDER OF THE GREAT VENETIAN SCHOOL

"*Giovanni Bellini was his name. Yet when people who loved beautiful pictures spoke of 'Gian,' every one knew who was meant, but to those who worked at art he was 'The Master.'* "—Hubbard.

❖

GIOVANNI, son of Jacopo and brother of Gentile Bellini, was born in Venice, Italy. His earliest known work is a Madonna, with a child standing before her on a parapet, painted in 1487, and now in the Academy in Venice. He frequently painted single figures of the Christ, marked by great nobility of expression, dignity of bearing and distinguished arrangement of draperies. A Madonna enthroned, with angels and four saints, in side-panels (1488) is in the sacristy of Santa Maria dei Frari in Venice. His works further include a *Transfiguration* (Naples Museum), *Peter Martyr* (National Gallery, Lindon), and *Baptism of Christ* (Santa Corona, Vincenza). His small pictures are gems of color, and have been the delight of artists for centuries. Giovanni Bellini had among his pupils Titian and Giorgione. He was really the progenitor of that school of colorists which made Venice famous in art. His work, particularly that of his later years (he lived to the age of ninety) was characterized by a greater freedom of touch than that of his predecessors, and by a richness and warmth of coloring which seems to have inspired Titian and many other great painters who succeeded him.

❖ ❖ ❖

Hubbard makes a Little Journey to Giovanni Bellini as a great painter and originator, who was equally great as a teacher and director. Famous among his pupils were Titian and Giorgione, who were deeply indebted to the elder Venetian master for their signal ability as colorists.

BOTTICELLI

Born 1447—Died 1510 Volume VI—Page 65

A GREAT VISIONARY PAINTER

"Botticelli and Rembrandt kept step in their history, both receiving instant recognition in early life and becoming rich. Then fashion and society turned against them—the tide of popularity began to ebb. Finally both begged alms in the public streets."—Hubbard.

❖

SANDRO FILIPEPI BOTTICELLI was born in Florence, Italy. The name Botticelli he took from a Florentine goldsmith under whom he first received instruction in draughtsmanship. His second master was the painter Fra Filippo Lippi, then at the height of his reputation. At twenty-two Botticelli was considered one of the first painters in Florence. About 1481 he was summoned to Rome by Pope Sixtus IV, to assist in painting his newly erected chapel in the Vatican. According to Vasari, he was made chief superintendent of the work, painting a number of the portraits of Popes in the upper niches of the chapel and three of the twelve frescoes. Botticelli returned to Florence about 1484, and subsequently became a disciple of the Dominican friar Fra Girolamo Savonarola. In his religious frenzy Sandro abandoned painting and was reduced to misery and want, according to Vasari. Nevertheless, surviving Savonarola, in 1500 Botticelli again took up his brush and painted one of his most beautiful religious pictures, *The Nativity*. Great as his reputation was for a time, he went out of favor and for three hundred years his work was not considered as a factor in the development of art. Living in a generation of naturalists, Botticelli was essentially a visionary painter. He was one of the first to accept art as an instrument of general culture and as much at the service of the world as of the Church. Except in one instance, he neither signed nor dated his works.

❖ ❖ ❖

Hubbard makes the Little Journey to Botticelli as an example of the eminently successful man whose boyhood showed little or no promise of future greatness. By his parents and early teachers he was given up as hopelessly handicapped by stupidity. Yet, thrown upon his own resources, Botticelli became a leading painter of Florence in his twenties.

MICHELANGELO

Born 1475—Died 1564 Volume IV—Page 5

GREAT PAINTER-SCULPTOR OF THE RENAISSANCE

"*Michelangelo gives one the impression of heroic strength, battling with fierce passions, and becoming victor over them . . . the mold of the man was masculine, and the subdued sorrow that flavors his whole career never degenerates into sickly sentimentality or repining.*"—Hubbard.

❖

MICHELANGELO BUONARROTI was born at Caprese, a Tuscan mountain town near Florence, Italy. In 1488 he began studying under the painter Ghirlandajo. Anticipating a civil war in Florence, in 1492 he went to Bologna, where he painted the well-known kneeling angel upon the arch of the Church of San Domenico. From 1496 to 1501 he lived in Rome, where he executed his famous *Bacchus* and *Cupid* in marble, followed by his great *Pietà di San Pietro*. Back in Florence, in 1501, he carved his great *David* of the Signoria, completed in 1504. In competition with Leonardo da Vinci he decorated the main hall of the Palazzo Vecchio with the great fresco, called the *Battle of Pisa*, which probably influenced Renaissance art more than any other single work. In 1505 he was called to Rome by Pope Julius II to design his mausoleum, the magnitude of which is evidenced by the colossal statue of *Moses*, the only feature of the project that Michelangelo carried out to his satisfaction. His great work on the ceiling of the Sistine Chapel at Rome occupied him from 1508 to 1512. Eight years later he executed the sacristy of San Lorenzo and decorated the tombs of the Medicis with the famous reclining figures of *Day and Night*, *Dawn and Twilight*, perhaps the most characteristic of all his works. Michelangelo spent six years (1535-41) painting *The Last Judgment* in the Sistine Chapel.

❖ ❖ ❖

The Little Journey to Michelangelo makes one realize how much is possible of accomplishment to the man who will maintain an open mind and go on learning to the end. Also that it is possible to achieve preëminent success in more than one direction. Michelangelo regarded himself as a sculptor, rather than a painter, and yet he painted what has been pronounced "the grandest picture in the world."

TITIAN

Born 1477—Died 1576 Volume IV—Page 147

THE GREAT VENETIAN PAINTER OF THE RENAISSANCE

"*Titian painted some dreary, commonplace pictures, and he also painted others that must ever be reckoned as among the examples of sublime art that have made the world stronger in its day and generation and proud of what has been.*"—Hubbard.

❖

TITIAN was born at Cadore, Italy. His family belonged to the minor nobility, his father being a magistrate and military commander. At nine, the lad was sent to Venice for instruction in art and letters, and studied under the Bellinis, having Giorgione and Palma Vecchio as fellow pupils. Titian developed slowly, and was approaching middle age before he was recognized as the master painter of Venice. In 1513 he was summoned to Rome by Pope Leo X, but preferring to remain in Venice, he petitioned the Senate to make him an official painter to the State. The petition was granted, together with a yearly pension of 300 crowns. To the period between 1513 and 1530 belong most of his great religious pictures, including the incomparable *Assumption of the Virgin.* As State painter he had the monopoly of portraying the Doges. His official portraits were destroyed in the fire of 1577, but many replicas survive. After losing his wife in 1530 Titian adopted a lavish mode of living and his home became the center of a famous literary and artistic circle, which even kings were glad to join. In 1532 he was summoned to Bologna to portray Charles V, and so pleased that monarch that he was named Court painter and his children were made nobles of the empire. In his hundredth year Titian fell a victim to the plague that ravaged Venice.

❖ ❖ ❖

In the Little Journey to Titian is traced the career of an eminently successful man who never suffered any serious reverses, maintaining habits of industry throughout a long life. Titian was fond of living, fond of the world. Feeling at home anywhere and everywhere, his secret of getting the most out of life was to keep busy and on the lookout for the bright side of things.

RAPHAEL

Born 1483—Died 1520 Volume VI—Page 11

THE MOST CELEBRATED PAINTER OF MODERN TIMES

"*Raphael marks an epoch. He did what no man before him had ever done, and by the sublimity of his genius placed the world forever under obligations to him. . . . Work, unceasing work, filled his days. The ingenuity and industry of the man were marvelous.*"—Hubbard.

❖

RAPHAEL SANTI was born at Urbino, Italy. Like his artist father, he enjoyed the favor of the Duke of Urbino, and was regarded as a remarkable painter before he became of age and went to Florence, in 1504. In Florence he learned perfect modeling and chiaro-oscuro from Leonardo da Vinci, improved his knowledge of anatomy and dramatic action through the study of Michelangelo, and from Fra Bartolommeo learned superior composition and the art of enlivening statuesque groups by contrast. His most original work of the Florentine period is the *Entombment of Christ* (Borghese Gallery, Rome). In 1508 his friend, the architect Bramante, induced Pope Julius II to summon Raphael to Rome to fresco four chambers of the Vatican, notably the Camera della Segnatura and the Stanza d'Eliodoro, which contain some of his most magnificent work. Before the death of Julius II in 1513, Raphael assumed an important position at the Papal Court, and under Leo X his influence increased. Upon the death of Bramante, in 1514, he was made chief architect of St. Peter's. The most powerful decorative work of his later life are the cartoons for the tapestries of the Sistine Chapel. As an architect Raphael was not of the same importance as a painter. His chief architectural work, aside from St. Peter's, is the Villa Madama (1516) which displays forms of simple majesty. Raphael died as the result of a fever contracted while directing excavations in Rome.

Raphael reached the pinnacle of fame and fortune at an age when most men are getting started. He experienced no reverses, made no enemies, was universally mourned when he died at thirty-seven. He is a rare example of the man who can dispense with the discipline of occasional setbacks in carving out a career.

CORREGGIO

Born 1494—Died 1534 Volume VI—Page 221

A GREAT ITALIAN PAINTER

"Correggio never painted his own portrait, and no one else seemed to consider him worth while; his income was barely sufficient for his wants. . . . Correggio struck thirteen because he was himself, and was to a great degree even ignorant and indifferent to what the world was doing." —Hubbard.

❖

ANTONIO ALLEGRI DA CORREGGIO was born in the Italian town after which he is named. His early years were passed there, and he acquired the rudiments of painting from his uncle, Lorenzo Allegri, and from Giambattista Lombardi, head of the academy at Correggio. In his earlier works are traces of the influence of Leonardo da Vinci. Following a sojourn of two years in Mantua, and a possible visit to Milan, Correggio returned to his native town and contracted to paint an altar-piece for the local Franciscan church. In 1518 he went to Parma in response to an invitation to decorate with frescoes the chamber of the Abbess of San Paolo. There he passed the greater part of his remaining life and painted his greatest works; there also he founded a school. Besides numerous easel works and altar-pieces, Correggio was engaged from 1520 to 1524 in painting the frescoes of the cupola of San Giovanni in Parma, and from 1526 to 1530 he adorned the great cupola of the cathedral. That done he returned to Correggio, where he lived out his days quietly and industriously painting mythological subjects. Marrying in 1520, his girl-wife is believed to have been the inspiration of three of his most charming Madonnas. She bore him four children. Correggio's place in the history of art is among the five great Italian painters, with Michelangelo, Leonardo, Raphael and Titian.

❖ ❖ ❖

A Little Journey is made to Correggio as a master painter who achieved greatness because he worked to please himself first and others afterward. This is cited by Hubbard as the best, if not only, recipe for the attainment of artistic success. The Correggios of mankind are those who concentrate their energies on doing the work they like best to do, regardless of the reward.

CELLINI

Born 1500—Died 1571 Volume VI—Page 273

EMINENT ITALIAN SCULPTOR AND GOLDSMITH

"Cellini had an intense personality; he was skilful as a workman; he told the truth as he saw it. . . . Cellini is not like us, and when we read his book we give thanks that we are not like him, but every trait that he had large, we have in little."—Hubbard.

❖

BENVENUTO CELLINI was born in Florence, Italy. As a result of a duel in which he was concerned he was forced to leave Florence, and circuitously made his way to Rome. Soon he attracted the attention of Pope Clement VII by his beautiful designs, becoming the greatest worker in precious metals of his time. He exercised his art for the aggrandizement of those who figured in the splendid society of the French and Italian Renaissance. Cellini was in Rome when it was besieged by the Constable de Bourbon, and, according to his own account, it was he who killed both the Constable and the Prince of Orange. For some years he divided his time between Florence and Rome, working at one period under Michelangelo. Francis I invited him subsequently to his Court, and Cellini stayed in France five years, becoming the recipient of a pension and title from the king. There he modeled the bronze relief of the *Nymph of Fontainebleau*, a fine specimen of his work. Returning to Florence, he found a patron in Cosima de Medici, for whom he fashioned the bronze statue of Perseus with the head of Medusa (now in the Loggia in Florence). In his fifty-eighth year he retired to a monastery and began to write his famous autobiography. But two years afterwards he resumed his reckless, energetic, but dissolute career, which ended in his natural death. He was buried in the Church of Santa Annunziata, Florence.

The importance of self-esteem as a factor in success is emphasized in the Little Journey to Benvenuto Cellini, whose autobiography is one of the classics of literature. As Hubbard states, "good healthy egotism in literature (or any other work, for that matter), is the red corpuscle that makes the thing live." In other words, one must be interested in oneself in order to be interesting to other people.

RUBENS

Born 1577—Died 1640 Volume IV—Page 81

CHIEF MASTER OF THE FLEMISH SCHOOL OF PAINTING

"*We may search long before finding a life so full to overflowing of material good things as that of Rubens. All he touched turned to gold. From the time he returned to Antwerp in Sixteen Hundred Eight to his death, his life-journey was one grand triumphal march.*"—Hubbard.

❖

PETER PAUL RUBENS was born at Siegen, Westphalia, and began his artistic training at the age of fifteen in Antwerp. The works of the great Italian colorists attracted him to Venice in 1600, and in the same year Duke Vincenzo of Gonzaga made him Court painter at Mantua. Sent to Rome in 1601 to make copies of old masters, Rubens also executed there, for Archduke Albert, Governor of the Netherlands, three altar-pieces in the Church of Santa Croce in Gerusalemme. In 1603 Gonzaga made him the bearer of gifts to King Philip III of Spain, whence he returned to Italy in 1604. The next few years he spent variously at Rome, Genoa and Milan, until he was recalled to Antwerp by his mother's illness. There he was appointed Court painter by Archduke Albert, and in 1609 he married. Masterpieces from his brush quickly succeeded each other, and students flocked to his studio in such numbers that he was obliged to refer applicants to other masters for years in advance. His painting was interrupted in 1627 by a diplomatic mission to London and Madrid to negotiate peace between England and Spain. This done, he was knighted by Charles I in 1630, and also by Philip IV of Spain. Long a victim of gout, the Flemish master succumbed to paralysis of the heart in his sixty-fourth year and was buried with great pomp in the Church of Saint Jacques, Antwerp.

❖ ❖ ❖

By turns an artist, a diplomat, a courtier, a horseman, a musician, Rubens carried every undertaking to a triumphant conclusion. Moreover, he found time to execute more pictures than any other painter in history. That quality need not be sacrificed to quantity is evidenced in the Little Journey to the versatile and industrious Flemish master.

ANTHONY VAN DYCK

Born 1599—Died 1641 Volume IV—Page 173

A FLEMISH MASTER PAINTER

"*Van Dyck's remains are buried in Saint Paul's Cathedral. A very fine monument, near the grave of Turner, marks the spot; but his best monument is in the examples of his work that are to be found in every great art-gallery of the world.*"—Hubbard.

❖

SIR ANTHONY VAN DYCK was born at Antwerp. At fifteen he became a pupil of Rubens. In 1620 he went to England and executed a full-length portrait of James I. In 1623, by the advice of Rubens, he went to Italy, sojourning first at Genoa, where he was welcomed by the resident Flemish painters. Here the best part of his life work begins. He was especially influenced by the great Venetian masters, producing works which in their splendor of color rivaled Titian. From Genoa he made short visits to Florence, Bologna, Venice and Rome. At Rome (1623) he was especially patronized by Cardinal Bentivoglio, whose fine portrait by Van Dyck hangs in the Pitti Palace. The date of his return to Antwerp is uncertain, but is thought to have been in 1626. In the meantime he probably visited Aix-la-Chapelle and Paris. His growing celebrity is attested by his appointment as Court painter to the Spanish regents of the Netherlands, Albert and Isabella. Invited to England in 1632 he was knighted by Charles I, named painter in ordinary to their Majesties and granted a yearly pension of £200. In 1641 he went to Paris, but was disappointed in his hopes of a commission to decorate the Louvre. In failing health he returned to London, where he died in his forty-first year.

❖ ❖ ❖

The career of Anthony Van Dyck, outlined in the Little Journey, illustrates the manner in which worldly and artistic success may be achieved simultaneously. Van Dyck was never even threatened with poverty, nor was his supremacy as a painter ever questioned. In fact, his death at forty was hastened by his unquestioned success.

VELASQUEZ

Born 1599—Died 1660 Volume VI—Page 155

FIRST OF THE OLD SPANISH MASTERS

"*Velasquez did not use his art to flatter: he had the artistic conscience. Truth was his guiding star. And the greatness of Velasquez is shown in that all subjects were equally alike to him. He did not select the classic or peculiar.*"—Hubbard.

❖

DIEGO RODRIGUEZ DE SILVA Y VELASQUEZ was a native of Seville, Spain, where he received his first schooling in both letters and art. He was fortunate in having as an early teacher, the painter Pacheco, whose influence is seen in the wonderful sureness of his drawing and the thoroughness of his work. In 1618 Velasquez married Pacheco's daughter, and in 1622 he went for the first time to Madrid. There he made the favorable acquaintance of Philip IV's all-powerful minister, Olivarez. Commissioned to paint an equestrian portrait of the King, Velasquez was so successful as to be appointed Court painter, with the exclusive privilege of portraying the King, and given a liberal pension and a studio in the Alcazar. The visit of Rubens as ambassador of Isabella, regent of the Netherlands, to Madrid, in 1628, was not without influence upon Velasquez. Rubens had a high opinion of the rising Spaniard and induced King Philip to let him spend eighteen months in Italy. Returning to Spain, Velasquez was Court painter from 1631 to 1649, doing much of his best work in that time. He revisited Italy in 1649 and executed a portrait of Pope Innocent X, which has been called "the greatest portrait of the seventeenth century." Again in Spain, he was appointed marshal of the palace, with a salary of 3,000 ducats and a home in the Alcazar. In 1659 he received the cross of Santiago, the highest honor attainable by a Spanish nobleman. He died of a fever at Madrid.

❖ ❖ ❖

Ordinary men can endure failure, which is a common experience, as Hubbard observes in the Little Journey to Velasquez, but to stand success over a long period of time, as Velasquez did, demands exceptional qualities. The struggle with adverse conditions helps most men to grow and develop, but here is a favorite of fortune who was not spoiled nor weakened by a constant succession of victories throughout his lifetime.

REMBRANDT

Born 1606—Died 1669 Volume IV—Page 41

THE GREAT DUTCH MASTER

"*Admiration did not spoil Rembrandt. His temperature was too low for ebullition—he took it all quite as a matter of course. His work was done with such ease that he was not aware it was extraordinary in quality.*"—Hubbard.

❖

REMBRANDT VAN RYN was born at Leyden, and first studied painting there and at Amsterdam, Holland. He was a precocious genius, and at twenty-five was the most fashionable and popular portrait painter in Amsterdam. Among his patrons were Frederick William, the Prince of Orange, and Burgomaster Jan Six; the foremost men of the day, like the poet Jeremiah Decker and Constantin Huygens, were his friends and associates. A portentous event in his life was his marriage in 1634 with Saskia van Ulenburgh, of a wealthy and influential Amsterdam family. Their happy union was the inspiration of many of his best works. After her death in 1642 he met with financial misfortunes and a pronounced falling-off in popularity. In 1657 his creditors sold his wonderful art collection, including several of his own paintings, for the pitiful sum of 500 florins, and in 1658 his house went for 1,100. He was adjudged a bankrupt, and died in poverty. Nevertheless the world has never produced a more original artist. His conceptions were essentially poetic and picturesque, but at the same time virile. The most prominent technical characteristic of his work is a marvelous rendition of light and shadow. Rembrandt exercised a profound influence upon the art of his day, and a more lasting one upon the art of the nineteenth century. In addition to his supremacy as a painter, he was probably the most consummate etcher of all time.

❖ ❖ ❖

Rembrandt furnishes an example of the fickleness of fortune and the instability of public favor. He enjoyed an immense popularity and saw it swiftly dwindle. The Little Journey to the great Dutch painter is a reminder, however, that by doing good work one is bound to win out in the long run.

JOSHUA REYNOLDS

Born 1723—Died 1792 Volume IV—Page 287

THE MOST CELEBRATED ENGLISH PORTRAIT PAINTER

"*A success so uninterrupted that it seems unequaled in the history of art. . . . He was generous and affectionate, wise and sincere; a cheerful and tireless worker—one in whom the elements were so well mixed that all the world might say, This was a man!*"—Hubbard.

❖

JOSHUA REYNOLDS was born at Plympton, Devonshire, England. Having manifested a desire to be a painter, he was, in 1741, placed under Hudson, the principal portrait painter of the day. In 1745 Reynolds opened a studio in London, but returned to his native town on the death of his father during the next year. He went to Italy in 1749 and spent three years studying the Italian masters to excellent effect. Upon his return to London in 1752 his works attracted great attention; and when the Royal Academy was instituted in 1768 he was elected president. He was knighted by George III, and succeeded Allan Ramsay as painter to the king in 1784. He founded the Literary Club (1764) for Dr. Samuel Johnson's benefit. To him Oliver Goldsmith dedicated his *Deserted Village*. Reynolds is estimated to have painted between two and three thousand portraits. They form an epitome of London society of the period. The National Gallery possesses a number of his best works, as also do the National Portrait Gallery (London), the Royal Academy and Oxford University. Although Sir Joshua preferred historical painting, his works of this character are less important. He was very prominent in the social world and lived in friendly intercourse with Johnson, Burke, Goldsmith, Gibbon, Garrick and other eminent men of his time.

❖ ❖ ❖

"To make it people's interest to advance you, by showing that their business will be better done by you than by any other person, is the only solid foundation of success; the rest is accident." So said Reynolds himself, and the observation characterizes the subject of the Little Journey to the Home of the most prolific portrait painter that ever lived.

GAINSBOROUGH

Born 1727—Died 1788 Volume VI—Page 129

GREAT BOTH AS A PORTRAIT AND LANDSCAPE PAINTER

"Gainsborough got his share, and more, of all those things which the world counts worth while. The gratitude of his heart was expressed by his life—generous, kind, joyous—never cast down except when he thought he had spoken harshly or acted unwisely—loyal to his friends, forgetting his enemies."—Hubbard.

❖

THOMAS GAINSBOROUGH, born at Sudbury, Suffolk, England, was the youngest of nine children, and self-supporting at eighteen years of age. His parents sent him to London at fifteen, to study painting and engraving. Returning to Sudbury in 1745, he devoted himself to landscape work, married and settled at Ipswich, where he remained fifteen years. In 1760 he removed to Bath, then at the height of its popularity as a fashionable watering resort, and painted many society leaders of the period. King George III invited him to Court, and gave him orders for portraits of himself and Queen. Thereafter his fame and prosperity were assured. In 1768 he was elected one of the original members of the Royal Academy. Gainsborough died in London, and was buried at his request in Kew Churchyard, without name or inscription on the stone that marked his grave. He painted simply that which charmed him in Nature, and was the first impressionist in landscape art, somewhat like Corot, interpreting her poetic qualities. The *Watering Place*, painted between 1768 and 1775, is considered one of his best landscapes; and the *Blue Boy*, his greatest work, is the portrait of a son of Jonathan Buttall, a wealthy London ironmonger. Of Gainsborough's three hundred paintings, two hundred and twenty are portraits; there are also a few etchings and a collection of his drawings in the British Museum.

❖ ❖ ❖

Gainsborough is a shining example of the man who goes ahead and does his work to the best of his ability, without regard to its importance or greatness. It is not surprising to observe in the Little Journey that this eminent artist was never fully satisfied with any of his pictures and was not accustomed to signing them. It is characteristic of such a person to take himself to task for not constantly doing better work.

THORWALDSEN

Born 1770—Died 1844 Volume VI—Page 95

EMINENT DANISH SCULPTOR

"Thorwaldsen should have tasted exile, poverty and heartbreak—not to have known these was his misfortune. And perhaps his best work lay in keeping alive the classic tradition; in educating whole nations to a taste for sculpture; in turning the attention of society from strife to art, from war to harmony."—Hubbard.

BERTEL THORWALDSEN was born at Copenhagen, and died there while on a visit from Rome, where he spent most of his artistic life. In 1793 he won the great gold medal at the Copenhagen Academy and three years later it was supplemented with a stipend sufficient to justify a journey to Rome. There he executed in marble his colossal statue of *Jason with the Golden Fleece* (1803), after which orders came in abundance. In 1804 he produced the famous group of *Cupid and Psyche* and the relief of *Dance of the Muses on Mount Helicon.* Coincidentally the Florence Academy appointed him professor, and in 1808 he was elected a member of the Academy of San Luca in Rome. About 1809 Thorwaldsen won a new patron in Crown Prince Louis of Bavaria, for whom he executed the statue of *Adonis,* not completed until 1832. Meanwhile he originated so many works between 1809 and 1811, some of them among his best, that he was obliged to have the help of his pupils. His life-size statue of *Psyche* is one of his master creations. Presently his frieze representing the *Entry of Alexander the Great Into Babylon* achieved a prodigious success, followed by many others, including the *Lion of Lucerne* and the colossal *Vulcan,* one of his last works done in Rome. In 1825 Thorwaldsen was elected president of the Academy of San Luca. His funeral was attended by the Danish royal family, and his monument is the Thorwaldsen Museum at Copenhagen.

That Thorwaldsen just missed being one of the greatest sculptors that ever lived is attributed by Hubbard to the misfortune of the Danish master in never having tasted the bitterness of failure in any important undertaking. "Good fortune attended him, even in circumstances that work havoc in most men's lives—he disarmed the Furies with a smile."

J. M. W. TURNER

Born 1775—Died 1851 Volume I—Page 123

THE GREAT ENGLISH LANDSCAPE PAINTER

"Turner's temperament was audacious, self-centered, self-reliant, eager for success and fame, yet at the same time scorning public opinion—a paradox often found in the artistic mind of the first class. . . . He was always the artist, never the realist."—Hubbard.

◆

JOSEPH M. W. TURNER was born in Covent Garden, London. His father was a barber, and was ambitious for his son to be an artist. In 1789 he studied under Reynolds, but was little influenced by him. His first picture exhibited at the Academy was of Lambeth Palace (1790). Subsequently he met Thomas Girtin, founder of modern water-color painting, with whom he sketched much and formed a fast friendship. His *Morning on the Comston Fells, Cumberland*, exhibited at the Academy in 1798, proclaimed his genius as a painter of poetic landscape. His *Battle of the Nile* (1799) made him an associate of the Royal Academy. As a result of his first visit to the Continent in 1802 he executed his *Calais Pier* and a *Holy Family*, followed by his famous *Shipwreck* and *Garden of the Hesperides* (1806). Between 1811 and 1815 Turner painted the *Apollo and Python*, *Hannibal and His Army Crossing the Alps* and *Dido Building Carthage.* Then ensued perhaps his best period (1820-35), represented by the wonderful Italian pictures upon which his fame chiefly rests, although some of his greatest pictures, such as the *Slave Ship*, remained to be done. After 1845 his mind and sight began to fail, but he was still at work when he died at Chelsea, leaving a fortune of £144,000 and 262 of his oil paintings, 135 watercolors, 1,757 studies in color and innumerable sketches.

❖ ❖ ❖

First the public scorned Turner. Then the tables were turned. Turner illustrates the fickleness of fame, if not fortune. He was called great in his own time, was rich, applauded, honored. Then came attack, death, defamation and such eclipse as required a Ruskin to dispel.

ARY SCHEFFER

Born 1795—Died 1858 Volume IV—Page 225

A FRENCH PAINTER OF THE ROMANTIC SCHOOL

"From the time he met the Princess of Orleans there came a decided evolution in his art; but it was not until she had passed away that one could pick out an unsigned canvas and say positively, 'This is Scheffer's.'"—Hubbard.

❖

ARY SCHEFFER was born at Dordrecht, Holland. He studied drawing at Lille, and in 1811 went to Paris, where, in the studio of Guérin, he had Géricault, and Delacroix for fellow students, and with them defied the ultra-classical teachings of Guérin. He preserved his connection with the new romantic movement in the expression of sentiment, but in execution Scheffer aimed more for purity of form. His life as an artist is divided into three periods. His attention was first attracted to scenes from real life, in depicting which he showed his sympathy with suffering, like *The Soldier's Widow*, and *Death of Géricault* (1824), now in the Louvre. His second period shows him absorbed in ideal scenes drawn from the work of Goethe and Schiller, Byron and Dante. In 1830 he painted the first of his series dealing with Marguerite, motivated by his sorrow over the death of his secret love, Princess Marie of Orleans. To this subject he frequently returned, the final one of the series, *Marguerite at the Fountain*, being painted in 1858. The third period, characterized by his religious subjects, is not distinctly marked off from the second, for he began the religious pictures with the *Christian Consolator* (1837). After 1840 he was largely occupied with sacred themes and reached his highest achievement in *Christ Weeping Over Jerusalem*, *Christ Tempted of Satan* and the *Christ of the Reed*.

❖ ❖ ❖

To make capital out of a loss or an affliction, is the lesson conveyed in the Little Journey to the Home of the French painter, Ary Scheffer, whose best work was done after the death of a woman whom he loved and mourned. It was the picture of her in his memory that he painted over and over and that stimulated his genius.

COROT

Born 1796—Died 1875 Volume VI—Page 187

GREATEST OF FRENCH LANDSCAPE PAINTERS

"When Camille Corot passed out, five thousand Paris art-students wore crape on their arms for a year in memory of a man who did his work joyously, lived long, and to the end carried in his heart the perfume of the morning and the beneficent beauty of the sunrise."—Hubbard.

❖

JEAN BAPTISTE CAMILLE COROT was born and died in Paris, France. After mastering the rudiments of painting, he spent the years 1825 to 1827 in Italy and made his debut at the French Salon with two Italian landscapes—a *View of Narni* and *Campagna at Rome.* He again went to Italy in 1834 and in 1842, besides traveling in France, Switzerland, the Netherlands and England. But the greater part of his life was passed near Paris at Ville d'Avray, in the forest of Fontainebleau and the valley of the Seine. In these places he found subjects for his most beautiful pictures. It was some time before his work was recognized, but in his later life honors were heaped upon him. He received medals in 1833, 1855 and 1857; in 1846 he received the Cross of the Legion of Honor, and in 1857 he was made a commander. The younger artists almost worshipped him, and in 1874 his friends gave him a gold medal to atone for the neglect of the Salon. Dealers clamored for his pictures, and his income was as much as 200,000 francs a year. But Corot cared little for money except to help his friends, which he did with a lavish hand. Gentle, jovial and kind, the artist never married, but was devotedly attached to his mother and his sister. Corot has been called the great lyric poet of the Barbizon School, as Rousseau was the epic and Dupré the dramatic.

As Hubbard observes of the foremost poet-painter of the nineteenth century, Corot is a remarkable example of a soul ripening slowly. His finest work was done when he was seventy-one years of age, and there was no decline in his powers during the eight years that followed. To cultivate a cheerful disposition and to await success patiently, is the lesson conveyed in the Little Journey to Corot.

LANDSEER

Born 1802—Died 1873 Volume IV—Page 311

AN EMINENT ENGLISH ANIMAL PAINTER

"Landseer's career was one of continuous prosperity. In his life there was neither tragedy nor disappointment. . . . He did a great work, and the world is better for his having lived; for his message was one of gentleness, kindness and beauty."—Hubbard.

❖

SIR EDWIN HENRY LANDSEER was born in London, and before he was twelve years of age could etch and paint in water-colors and oil. He made his début at the Royal Academy Exhibition in 1815. From then on his paintings attracted increasing attention, beginning with his *Fighting Dogs* (1819) and *Alpine Mastiffs Reviving a Traveler in the Snow* (1820). The latter work, engraved by his father and brother, became one of the most popular prints of the day. In 1825 he went to Scotland, visiting Sir Walter Scott, whom he painted with his dogs at Abbotsford, and traveling in the Highlands. This visit was of decisive influence upon his art. From this time he began to paint animals, especially the dog, in their relation to man, endowing them with human sentiments. He also increased the popularity of his pictures by carefully chosen names. Landseer became an associate of the Royal Academy in 1826, at the earliest age allowed by the statutes, and a member in 1831. He frequently drew and painted Queen Victoria and Albert, the Prince Consort, both of whom he taught etching. In 1850 he was knighted, and five years later he received gold medals at the Paris Exposition, and at Vienna in 1873. In 1865 he declined the presidency of the Academy. His works are best known through the large number of engravings made of them, especially by his brother Thomas.

The Little Journey to Landseer points the way to attaining success by being always agreeable and arousing no antagonisms. His great popularity as a painter was largely owing to his deference to the spirit of the age in which he lived and worked. His career furnishes proof that it pays better to make friends than to make enemies—and costs no more.

FRANÇOIS MILLET

Born 1814—Died 1875 Volume IV—Page 259

A GREAT FRENCH GENRE AND LANDSCAPE PAINTER

"Jean François Millet is to art what Wagner is to music, or what Whitman is to poetry. . . . They were all revolutionaries; and success came so tardily to them that flattery did not taint their native genius." —Hubbard.

❖

JEAN FRANÇOIS MILLET was born at Gruchy, near Cherbourg, France. His father was a peasant who, however, encouraged the boy to study art. In 1837, aided by a small pension granted by the town council of Cherbourg, Millet went to Paris and studied under Delaroche. The conventional style of that master was repellant to him and he opened a little studio of his own, supporting himslf mainly by painting cheap portraits and pastel imitations of Boucher and Watteau. He won some recognition with a portrait in the Salon of 1840, but soon returned to Normandy, where he married (1841). In 1842 he went back to Paris, and two years later attracted favorable attention by his *Milkwoman* and *Riding Lesson.* Not until 1848 did he achieve a real success, with *The Winnower.* In that year he settled in the village of Barbizon, near Paris, and there passed the rest of his life painting the revolutionary rustic subjects on which his fame rests. *The Sower* (1850) was followed by *The Reapers* (1853), *The Gleaners* (1857), *The Angelus* (1859). In 1860 he contracted to give all his work for three years for 1,000 francs a month, but the contract was dissolved in six months. To this period belong *The Sheep Shearing, Potato Planters* and *The Man With the Hoe* (1863). Driven from Barbizon by the Franco-Prussian War, Millet repaired to Cherbourg and did not return to Paris until 1871. He continued to paint until a few weeks before his death.

❖ ❖ ❖

To succeed at a given undertaking too easily is apt to give one a false idea of the value of true success. Millet furnishes an example of the benefits one may derive from having to struggle through the better part of a lifetime to reach a definite goal. The Little Journey to Millet serves as a reminder that it is better to succeed late than too early in life.

MEISSONIER

Born 1815—Died 1891 Volume IV—Page 119

A GREAT FRENCH GENRE PAINTER

"Meissonier was a natural artist: he saw things clearly and in detail; he had the heart to feel, and he longed for the skill to express that which he saw and felt. And when the desire is strong enough it brings the thing —and thus is prayer answered."—Hubbard.

❖

JEAN LOUIS ERNEST MEISSONIER was born at Lyons, France. His parents removed to Paris when he was a lad, and there, in 1830, he began to study art, supporting himself by etching and illustration work. His first painting to be exhibited at the Salon was *The Visitors*, 1836. In 1843 and 1848 he received first-class medals from the Salon, and in the expositions of 1855, 1867 and 1878 the grand medal of honor. In 1848 he was captain of artillery in the National Guards. He was with Napoleon III at Solferino in 1859, and during the siege of Paris in 1870 he was lieutenant-colonel of infantry in the National Guards. He was made chevalier of the Legion of Honor in 1846 and grand officer in 1878; a member of the Institute of France in 1861, and a president in 1876 and 1891. As Hubbard observes, Meissonier rarely painted pictures of women or children, his characters being almost entirely men. He excels in his drawing of the horse, in his portrayal of action, and in his power to depict the subtlest shades of expression on the faces of his characters. Of his military pictures, one of the most famous is *Friedland or* 1807 (1875), a large canvas in the Metropolitan Museum, New York. Other famous pictures of his are *Cavalry Charge* (1867); *Napoleon III at Solferino* (1864) in the Luxembourg; *The Retreat from Moscow*, *Napoleon Overlooking a Battle*, *Napoleon and His Staff in* 1814.

Meissonier is revealed in the Little Journey as never hesitating to erase a whole picture when it did not satisfy his inward sense—critics might praise and customers offer to buy, it made no difference. "I have some one who is more difficult to please than you," he would say; "I must satisfy myself."

Rosa Bonheur

Born 1822—Died 1899 Volume II—Page 135

The Most Eminent Woman Animal Painter

"All the honors the Salon could bestow were heaped upon the young woman, and by special decision all her work henceforth was declared exempt from examination by the Jury of Admission. Rosa Bonheur, five feet four, weighing one hundred twenty pounds, was bigger than the Salon."—Hubbard.

❖

MARIE ROSA BONHEUR was born in Bordeaux, France. Her father, who was a drawing teacher, gave her careful training at an early age; but her genius was developed mainly by her own study of animals in their natural environments. The family moved to Paris when Rosa was eleven years old, and she copied industriously in the Louvre and the Luxembourg. The family studio has been described as a kind of Noah's Ark. At nineteen Mlle. Bonheur first exhibited at the Salon a picture of *Rabbits Eating Carrots.* Thereafter, until 1855, she was represented annually in the exhibition, receiving gold medals in 1845 and 1849. Her first great picture, deemed by some her best, *Ploughing in the Nivernais,* was bought for the Luxembourg in 1849. Four years later she exhibited the famous *Horse Fair,* and offered it to her native city for 12,000 francs. The offer was declined, and she sold it in England for 40,000 francs. Later it was purchased by Cornelius Vanderbilt for the Metropolitan Museum of Art in New York for $55,500. Rosa Bonheur bought a chateau at By, near Fontainebleau, in 1850. There, in 1864, Napoleon III and the Empress Eugenie visited her studio, and in the following year the Empress conferred upon the artist the Cross of the Legion of Honor, the first time a woman had been thus distinguished.

❖ ❖ ❖

Rosa Bonheur is made the subject of a Little Journey not only because she remains the foremost woman painter of animals, but because she was a pioneer of her sex in proving that women could successfully compete with men in the arts, as well as in the professions and in business.

GUSTAVE DORÉ

Born 1833—Died 1883 Volume IV—Page 329

A GREAT FRENCH ILLUSTRATOR

"*Gustave Doré drew pictures because he could do nothing else. He never had a lesson in his life, never drew from a model, could not sketch from nature. . . . He produced over one hundred thousand sketches, made two million dollars, was knighted, flattered, proclaimed, hooted, maligned, and died broken-hearted.*"—Hubbard.

❖

PAUL GUSTAVE DORÉ was born at Strassburg, France. So precocious was he that at ten he made sketches for lithographs, and in his fifteenth year was regularly employed as an illustrator in Paris and exhibited pen sketches in the Salons. His Rabelais illustrations, which appeared in 1854, established his reputation, and this work was followed by an incredible number of others, equally famous. He was not only popular in France, but in the United States and throughout Europe, especially in England, where there was a Doré cult. He worked with amazing facility and fecundity, acquiring great sums of money through his art. He was made a Chevalier of the Legion of Honor in 1861, and Officer in 1879. His chief masterpieces of engraving, besides the *Rabelais*, are *Don Quixote* (1863) and Dante's *Inferno* (1861). Among the numerous other works which he illustrated were Balzac's *Droll Stories*, the Bible, La Fontaine's *Fables*, Milton's *Paradise Lost*, Tennyson's *Idylls of the King*, Coleridge's *Ancient Mariner* and Poe's *Raven*. Doré aspired to be a historical painter, and, with his accustomed facility, created many works, mostly of colossal proportions. Among them are *Christ Leaving the Prætorium* and *Christ's Entry Into Jerusalem*. He died in Paris.

❖ ❖ ❖

In the Little Journey to Doré we are in contact with the type of individual who must do things in his own way in order to do them satisfactorily or at all. Such a person cannot be taught by another, but must learn from experience to proceed in the direction he is most strongly inclined to take.

WHISTLER

Born 1834—Died 1903 Volume VI—Page 329

THE MOST DISTINCTIVE AMERICAN PAINTER

"Whistler is an artist, and the soul of the man is revealed in his work—not in his hat, nor yet his bamboo cane, nor his long black coat, much less the language which he uses, Talleyrand-like, to conceal his thought. Art has been his life, his children and his religion."—Hubbard.

❖

JAMES A. McNEILL WHISTLER was born at Lowell, Massachusetts, the son of a distinguished army engineer. His cultured mother was the constant companion and instructor of his boyhood. In 1842 the lad accompanied his parents to Russia, where his father engaged in the construction of the first railroad between St. Petersburg (now Leningrad) and Moscow. Returning to America, in 1851 Whistler entered West Point, where his ability as a draughtsman did not make up for his inattention to other studies, with the result that he was dismissed. Following a period of art study in Paris, from 1857 to 1863 his pictures were refused at the Salon, but his *Little White Girl* achieved a signal success in the Salon des Refusés. As an etcher his *Thames Series* (1871) placed him in the first rank, made more secure by his *First and Second Venice Series* (1880-81). The eccentricities of Whistler and his quarrels with English artists and critics during his residence in London (1858-90) attracted more attention than his paintings, especially his famous quarrel with Ruskin. It was then, however, that he executed his principal works, including the *Artist's Mother*, now in the Louvre. In 1887 he was elected president of the Royal Society of British Artists, resigning in 1889. He became an Officer of the Legion of Honor in 1891, and divided his last years between Paris and London.

❖ ❖ ❖

The great lesson that Whistler has taught the world is to observe—to see things by and for oneself and, incidentally, to picture them. His other important teaching, as Hubbard points out, is that of selection—what to omit, what to keep and make use of.

FORTUNY

Born 1839—Died 1874 Volume IV—Page 201

A Great Spanish Painter and Etcher

"Fortuny's life is mirrored in his name: his whole career was one triumphant march to fortune, fame, love and honor. . . . He accomplished remarkable results, but all this splendid work he regarded as merely in the line of preparation for a greater work yet to come."—Hubbard.

❖

MARIANO JOSE Y CARBO was born at Réus in Catalonia, Spain, and died in Rome. He studied at the academy in Barcelona, and in 1856 won a prize which enabled him to pursue his studies in Italy. During the Spanish war against Morocco (1859-60) he was on the staff of General Prim, but spent most of his time sketching Oriental subjects. With a view to copying the Spanish masters he went, in 1865, to Madrid, where he fell under the influence of Goya. There he made the acquaintance of the painter Madrazo, whose daughter he married. In 1866 he visited Paris and received commissions that enabled him to settle in Rome, where he spent the remainder of his life. Fortuny thenceforth made a specialty of kaleidoscopic pictures of the Rococo period. His studio was a salon in which men of letters, artists and social leaders were wont to congregate. His canvases are usually of small dimension, but are filled with multitudinous details painted with great freedom, skill and vivacity of coloring. He is most successful with dazzling sunlight effects. The city hall of Barcelona contains several of his paintings, notably the *Battle of Tetuan*, considered one of his finest works, although unfortunately not finished. There is a large number of his works in America, both in public and private possession. Fortuny was also an acquarellist of note, and a brilliant etcher.

❖ ❖ ❖

The Little Journey to Fortuny serves as a warning to procrastinators. The life of this great Spanish artist was suddenly cut short in his thirty-sixth year, when he was still getting ready to do what he planned to be his biggest work. Nevertheless, he accomplished enough in his brief but busy life to rank him with the master painters of the world.

ABBEY

Born 1852—Died 1911 Volume VI—Page 305

A Great American Painter

Edwin A. Abbey seems to be the perfect type of man, who by doing all his work well, with no vaulting ambitions, has placed himself right in the line of evolution—evolving into something better, stronger and nobler all the time."—Hubbard.

❖

EDWIN AUSTIN ABBEY was born in Philadelphia and died in London, England. He first studied at the Philadelphia Academy of Fine Arts, and afterward worked as a magazine illustrator in New York until 1883, when he removed to England. In painting he has produced important canvases, dealing with subjects taken from Shakespeare, among other poets, and from romantic story. One of his most important works, which admirably combines deep intellectual and spiritual qualities, are the famous panels of the *Search for the Holy Grail*, on the upper walls of the delivery room of the Boston Public Library. Abbey has also produced some very individual work in pastel, full of sentiment and color. His works are distinguished by careful archæological accuracy and fine sentiment. His strong feeling for color is remarkable in one who passed so many years as a worker in black and white. He is ranked among the strongest colorists and the most intellectual painters of America. Abbey was chosen a member of the Royal Academy in 1898; was one of the American jurors on paintings in the Paris Exposition of 1900; and was commissioned by Edward VII to paint the coronation scene in Westminster Abbey. He married, in 1890, Miss Mary Mead of New York, who survived him. Though many years a resident of England Abbey never abandoned his American nationality.

"Give me a little time," Abbey is quoted, in the Little Journey, as saying of his great work in the Boston Public Library, "and I'll do something worth while." The remark is characteristic of the man who is never entirely pleased with what he has done, no matter what others may say, but is hopeful and confident of being able to do better.

BOOK SIX

❖

MUSIC AND POETRY

JOHN MILTON

Born 1608—Died 1674 Volume V—Page 119

ENGLAND'S GREAT EPIC POET

"*Milton was married to his work. He traversed the vast fields of classic literature, read in the original from Greek, Hebrew, Syriac, French, Spanish, Latin and Italian. He delved into abstruse mathematics, studied music as a science, and labored at theology.*"—Hubbard.

❖

JOHN MILTON was born and died in London, where his father was a prosperous scrivener. Graduating from Cambridge University, he passed six years on his father's estate in Buckinghamshire, reading the classics and writing poetry. Believing that he was destined to be a great poet, he went to Italy in 1638 to fit himself more fully for his life work. For some time he stayed in Florence, where he visited in prison the blind Galileo. Returning to London in 1639, he was drawn into ecclesiastical controversies, and wrote many pamphlets. In 1643 he married, after a brief courtship, the seventeen-year-old daughter of an Oxfordshire squire and royalist. She died in 1652, leaving him four children. Shortly after the execution of Charles I (1649) Milton issued a memorable defense of the deed and became widely known as a controversialist. On the establishment of the Commonwealth he was appointed Latin secretary to the Council of State. In 1652 he became blind, and four years later took a second wife, who inspired one of his finest sonnets. She died in 1658. The Restoration put an end to his political career, and in 1663 Milton acquired a house in Artillery Walk, Bunhill Fields, London, his last residence. There he married a third wife, thirty years his junior, and completed and published *Paradise Lost.*

❖ ❖ ❖

In the Little Journey to Milton we have an illustration of the man who spends the best years of his life preparing himself for a particular work. Milton never doubted his ability to write an epic poem—and "Paradise Lost" is the result of his confidence and determination.

SEBASTIAN BACH

Born 1685—Died 1750 Volume XIV—Page 135

FOUNDER OF GERMAN MUSIC

"*What Shakespeare is to literature, Michelangelo to sculpture, and Rembrandt to portrait painting, Johann Sebastian Bach is to organ-music. He was the greatest organist of his time, and his equal has not yet been produced, though nearly three hundred years have passed since his death.*"—Hubbard.

❖

JOHANN SEBASTIAN BACH was born at Eisenach, Thuringia. As the organ was to be his instrument *par excellence*, it is interesting to note that his serious study of it began in Lüneberg, which he left in 1703 to become a member of the band of Prince Johann Ernest at Weimar. In 1707 he accepted the position of organist of the principal church at Mühlhausen with a substantial salary and "the accustomed dues of corn, wood and fish." There he married and remained a twelvemonth before becoming organist of the Ducal Chapel at Weimar, where he spent nine productive years. In 1717 he accepted from Prince Leopold of Anhalt-Köthen the office of kapellmeister, and his sojourn there is distinguished for his chamber music as the Weimar period is for his organ compositions. At Köthen his first wife died and Bach found a second wife in a singer at the Ducal Court. Both his marriages were happy. Bach was the father of twenty children. In 1723 he became Musical Director of Leipzig, where he produced one of his greatest works, *The Passion According to Saint Matthew*. In 1747 occurred his famous meeting with Frederick the Great, for whom Bach wrote his *Musical Offering*. On his deathbed Bach wrote *Herewith I Come Before Thy Throne*. His funeral was inauspicious, and his grave has been obliterated.

❖ ❖ ❖

A Little Journey is made to Sebastian Bach as a great musician who simply developed the powers that were natural to him and who never thought of himself as being destined for immortality.

GEORGE HANDEL

Born 1685—Died 1759 Volume XIV—Page 251

AN EMINENT ANGLO-GERMAN COMPOSER

"Like the soul of John Brown, the spirit of Handel goes marching on. And Sir Arthur Sullivan was right when he said, 'Musical England owes more to Father Handel than to any other ten men who can be named—he led the way for us all.'"—Hubbard.

❖

GEORGE FREDERICK HANDEL was born at Halle, Germany. He received but slight instruction in music prior to taking a position in the orchestra of the Hamburg Opera House in 1703. There he soon astonished the public by his skill at the harpsichord during the temporary absence of the renowned Keiser. At the age of twenty he produced his first opera, *Almira*. Visiting Italy, Handel produced in Florence the opera *Roderigo*, and in Venice *Agrippina*, both of which were received with enthusiasm. In 1710 Handel went to England, where he spent practically the rest of his life and where his opera *Rinaldo* was the first of many successes. The year 1713 saw the production of his *Te Deum* and *Jubilate*, in celebration of the Peace of Utrecht. They brought him a life pension of £200. Between 1720 and 1740 Handel produced more than a score of excellent operas, and he would have been uninterruptedly prosperous had he not been ambitious to be an opera producer as well as composer. In 1739 he produced *Saul*, followed by *Israel in Egypt*, which many consider superior to his famous *Messiah*, produced in 1741. At its first London performance, when the *Hallelujah Chorus* was reached, the King and the whole audience rose, thus establishing a custom which continues to this day. Toward the end of his life Handel became blind, but continued to accompany his oratorios on the organ. He is buried in Westminster Abbey.

Handel is representative of that numerous class of men who are not satisfied with succeeding in what they can do best, but are ever venturing on a hazard of new fortunes. What Handel won as a composer he lost as a producer. However, as Hubbard says, "At fifty-five a bankrupt, Handel pays off every shilling with interest and celebrates the event by writing *Saul*, the Dead March from which will never die."

OLIVER GOLDSMITH

Born 1728—Died 1774 Volume I—Page 273

AN ESTEEMED IRISH POET AND PLAYWRIGHT

"Dear little Doctor Goldsmith, you were not a hustler, but when I get to the Spirit-World, I'll surely hunt you up!"—Hubbard.

❖

OLIVER GOLDSMITH was born in the village of Pallas, County of Longford, Ireland, and died in London, where he was buried in the Temple Churchyard. When six years old, Oliver was placed in the village school kept by an old soldier, Thomas Byrne, described in *The Deserted Village*. He graduated from Trinity College, Dublin, in 1749. An uncle, who had financed his education, gave him £50 to study law in London, but Goldsmith lost it in a Dublin gaming-house. Eventually he studied medicine in Edinburgh, went tramping over Europe, and in 1756 settled in London and began to practice medicine. From this he turned to literature, with what success may be gathered from the fact that when he was nominated physician and surgeon in the India service and failed to pass the examination, the very clothes in which he appeared before the examiners were borrowed; and being in great distress, he pawned them. In 1764 the famous Literary Club was founded in London, with Goldsmith as one of the nine original members. He published in chronological order *The Traveler*, which established him as a poet; *The Vicar of Wakefield*, his only novel; *The Good-Natured Man*, a play; *The Deserted Village*, his finest poem; and his great comedy, *She Stoops To Conquer*. His monument in Westminster Abbey bears an epitaph by Dr. Samuel Johnson.

❖ ❖ ❖

A Little Journey is made to Oliver Goldsmith as an author who endeared himself to the world, not only because of his literary creations but because of his improvidence. That worldly prosperity is rarely the reward of a literary artist of the first order is shown in the career of Goldsmith.

Wolfgang Mozart

Born 1756—Died 1791 Volume XIV—Page 299

Co-founder of German Opera

"In all the realm of artistic history no record of such extremes can be found in one life as those seen in the life of Mozart. . . . Mozart not only won the nod of nobility, and the favor of the highest in his own land, but he captured Italy . . . in his thirteenth and fourteenth years."—Hubbard.

❖

WOLFGANG MOZART was born at Salzburg, Austria. When only five years old he composed minuets and was at work on a concerto. At six he was such a proficient performer that his father took him and an elder sister on a successful tour of the leading capitals of Europe. In 1768 the boy conducted a solemn mass of his own composition at Vienna, and his operetta *Bastien and Bastienne* was given at a private performance. The following two years were spent in Italy, where his compositions and performances made such an impression that the Pope created him a Knight of the Golden Spur, and at Bologna he was elected a member of the Philharmonic Society. At Milan he was commissioned to compose the opera *Mitridate re di Ponto*, produced in 1770. During the next year he brought out his serenata *Ascanio in Alba*, in honor of the nuptials of Archduke Ferdinand, a son of Maria Theresa. Other works followed rapidly until the production of the opera *Idomeneo* at Munich opened a new epoch in his life, being his first masterpiece in the grand style. In 1782 his marriage to Constance Weber was signalized by the production in Vienna of his *Belmonte und Constanza*, followed by *Il nozze di Figaro*. A few months after the production of *The Magic Flute*, and while at work on his *Requiem*, Mozart died in his thirty-sixth year.

In the Little Journey to Mozart we have a perfect illustration of the eminently successful artist who, through improvidence and impracticality, is always in the toils of poverty. As Hubbard observes of Mozart, "He was always composing, making plans, seeing the silver tint in the clouds, but all of his music was taken by this one or that in whom he foolishly trusted, and only debt and humiliation followed him."

ROBERT BURNS

Born 1759—Died 1796 Volume V—Page 93

THE GREAT LYRIC POET OF SCOTLAND

"Robert Burns wrote some deathless lines—lines written out of the freshness of his heart, simply to please himself, with no furtive eye on Dumfries, Edinburgh, the Kirk or the Unco Guid of Ayrshire; and these are the lines that have given him his place in the world of letters."—Hubbard.

❖

ROBERT BURNS was born at Alloway, in Ayrshire, Scotland, and died at Dumfries. He was the eldest son of William Burness, a nurseryman, whose ancestors had long been farmers in Kincardineshire, and Agnes, the daughter of a Carrick farmer. He received a meager education, and in 1783, in conjunction with his brother Gilbert, rented a farm at Mossgiel, whither he removed in the following year. He published a volume of poems at Kilmarnock in 1786, on which occasion he changed the spelling of his family name to Burns. He had begun writing verses, however, ten years previously, his first poem being addressed to Nelly Kilpatrick, by whose side he had worked in the fields. It was at Mossgiel that he wrote some of his finest poems, such as the *Cottar's Saturday Night*, *The Jolly Beggars* and the lines *To a Mouse*. The success of his first volume and negotiations for a second drew him to Edinburgh, where he was lionized socially and made a favorable impression by the "dignified plainness and simplicity" of which Scott, who then saw him, speaks. From the second edition of his poems he realized about £500. In 1788 he married Jean Armour, by whom he had previously had several children. He took a farm at Ellisland in the same year, and in 1789 became an officer of the excise. In 1791 he removed to Dumfries, where he passed the last five years of his life.

Hubbard observes of Burns that he succeeded as a lover and as a poet, but failed in everything else. The thought conveyed in the Little Journey to Burns is that it is better to succeed positively in one or two things than to make a half-way success of many undertakings.

LUDWIG VAN BEETHOVEN

Born 1770—Died 1827 Volume XIV—Page 223

A GREAT GERMAN COMPOSER OF DUTCH DESCENT

"*Art was Beethoven's solace. Art is harmony, beauty and excellence. The province of art is to impart a sublime emotion. Beethoven's heart was filled with divine love—and all love is divine—and through his art he sought to express his love to others.*"—Hubbard.

❖

LUDWIG VAN BEETHOVEN was a native of Bonn, Germany. A precocious genius, in 1784 he was appointed second Court organist in the Chapel of the Elector of Cologne, who, in 1787, paid his expenses to Vienna. There he met Mozart, who, after hearing his play, predicted a great career for him. At Vienna he studied under Haydn, and there exist over 200 of his exercises, 42 of which Haydn corrected. In 1794 Beethoven, dissatisfied with the lack of attention given him by Haydn, who went to England in that year, took lessons from Albrechtsberger and from Schuppanzigh on the violin. He published his three trios, known as Opus I, in 1795, and from then on published his compositions with regularity. In 1802 his deafness, which had long been approaching, began to be serious. Nevertheless, his productiveness was amazing. Among the works produced during his first years of deafness are the pianoforte sonata with the familiar funeral march, the so-called *Moonlight Sonata* (not thus named by Beethoven); the *Second Symphony;* the *Kreutzer Sonata* for piano and violin; the *Eroica Symphony* (3rd); the *Waldstein* and *Appassionata* sonatas, and in 1805 his opera *Fidelio,* revised in 1806 and 1814. Beethoven made his last public appearance in 1816. He died during a terrific thunderstorm, and his last recorded words were, "I shall hear in heaven."

❖ ❖ ❖

To have been deaf and yet one of the greatest music composers who ever lived, was the distinction of Beethoven. He furnishes a notable example of fortitude and a determination to make the most of a crippled life. "I will grapple with fate; it shall never drag me down," Beethoven declared.

WILLIAM WORDSWORTH

Born 1770—Died 1850 Volume I—Page 211

A CELEBRATED ENGLISH POET

"Wordsworth's service to humanity consists in the fact that he has shown us old truth in a new light, and has made plain the close relationship that exists between physical nature and the soul of man."—Hubbard.

❖

WILLIAM WORDSWORTH was born at Cockermouth, Cumberland, England, and died at Rydal Mount in Westmoreland. He was educated at Hawkshead and at St. John's College, Cambridge, where he graduated in 1791. He spent some time in European travel and became an ardent republican. Later, however, he became a stanch conservative, if not Tory, and was severely criticized by Byron and by Browning in *The Lost Leader*. He received a legacy in 1795, and with his sister Dorothy settled at Racedown, Dorset. A visit from Coleridge in 1797 determined his career, and in the next year he removed to Alfoxden in Somerset to be near him. Following a sojourn in Europe, Wordsworth settled at Grasmere, in the Lake District. In 1798 he and Coleridge published *Lyrical Ballads*, to which Wordsworth contributed *Simon Lee*, *We Are Seven*, *Expostulation and Reply*, and *Lines on Tintern Abbey*. The book marks an epoch in the history of English poetry. In 1802 Wordsworth married Mary Hutchinson, and for nearly fifty years devoted himself to "plain living and high thinking." He was appointed distributor of stamps for Westmoreland in 1813, a post that paid £400 a year. This was supplemented by a Government pension of £300 in 1842; and in the ensuing year he succeeded Southey to the laureateship. His grave is in Grasmere churchyard.

❖ ❖ ❖

Wordsworth, like Tennyson, his successor to the English laureateship, and like his critic Browning, consecrated his life to poetry. Taking as his theme that the life of the flower and of man have the same origin and that they are akin, Wordsworth shows what can be done with one idea. That is the fundamental theme of all his poetry.

SAMUEL T. COLERIDGE

Born 1772—Died 1834 Volume V—Page 289

ENGLISH POET, SEER AND CRITIC

"*He taught men to think and separate truth from error. He was not popular, for he did not adapt himself to the many. His business was to teach teachers—he conducted a Normal School, and taught teachers how to teach.*"—Hubbard.

❖

SAMUEL TAYLOR COLERIDGE was born at Ottery Saint Mary, Devonshire, England, and was educated at Christ's Hospital, London, where Charles Lamb was a schoolfellow, and at Cambridge. In 1795 a Bristol bookseller offered Coleridge thirty guineas for a volume of his poems, and promised him a guinea and a half for every hundred lines he should write subsequently. On this prospect he married Sara Ficker, to whose sister Robert Southey was engaged. His *Juvenile Poems* appeared in 1796. Late in that year he settled at Nether Stowey, whither Wordsworth removed in the following year. Relieved of material cares by an annuity from two admirers, Coleridge there composed his finest poems, including *The Ancient Mariner*, the first part of *Christabel* and *Kubla Khan.* In 1798 was published the epoch-making *Lyrical Ballads*, of which Coleridge and Wordsworth were co-authors. Through the generosity of Cambridge classmates Coleridge spent nearly a year in Germany, returning to England to reside near Wordsworth and Southey and Keswick, in the Lake district of Westmoreland. Several publishing ventures were abortive, but in 1813 his play *Remorse* was successfully produced in London. Coleridge was an opium victim during the latter years of his life. In him were eminently united the three functions of critic, philosopher and poet.

Having done his life work before he was thirty, Coleridge was too exhausted to accomplish anything of importance during the last thirty years of his existence. "I should have died, like Keats, in youth and not have made myself a burden," he regrets, in the Little Journey. Nature endows us with just so much capital to start with, and to spend it too quickly is to invite bankruptcy.

ROBERT SOUTHEY

Born 1774—Died 1843 Volume V—Page 265

AN ENGLISH POET LAUREATE

"No taint of excess or folly marks the name of Southey; his life was filled with good works and kind deeds. His name is honored by a monument in the village of Keswick, and in Crosthwaite Church is another monument to his memory, the inscription being written by Wordsworth." —Hubbard.

❖

ROBERT SOUTHEY was born at Bristol, England, where his father was a linen draper. In 1788 he was sent to Westminster School, from which he was expelled four years later, on account of an essay against flogging. After two years at Oxford, he met Coleridge and they became brothers-in-law through their marriage to Edith and Sara Fricker at Bristol. In 1803 the Southeys and Coleridges settled at Keswick, in the Lake district of Westmoreland. Here, at Greta Hall, Southey passed the rest of his life in literary pursuits. Besides the income from his pen, which eventually became large, he received an annuity of £160 from a wealthy school friend, and later a Government pension of £300. In 1813 he was appointed poet laureate of England. In this capacity he wrote *The Vision of Judgment* (1821), an apotheosis of George III, which was brilliantly parodied by Byron. Southey became a widower in 1837, and two years later he married Caroline Anne Bowles, who had solicited his opinion of a poem she had written. During the year 1839 Southey became demented, dying afterward of softening of the brain. In unflagging literary industry Southey was one of the notable figures of his time. His prose, far more than his poetry, is a contribution of permanent value to English letters.

That a poet and man of letters can work as hard and steadfastly as the next person, and shoulder responsibility as cheerfully, is shown in the Little Journey to Southey. Faced with the problem of supporting his own and Coleridge's families with his pen, Southey did not shirk the task, but succeeded in making literature pay him handsomely. Southey illustrates the fact that industry can be made to take the place of genius on occasion.

PAGANINI

Born 1782—Died 1840

Volume XIV—Page 49

GREATEST OF VIOLINISTS

"As a violinist Paganini far surpassed all other players who ever lived. . . . Such patience, such persistency, such painstaking effort as the man put forth for a score of years would have made him master of anything." —Hubbard.

❖

NICCOLÒ PAGANINI was a native of Genoa, Italy. At an early age he resolved to be a great violinist, and succeeded in his ambition through rigorous and incessant practise. He produced his first sonata before he was nine years of age, and made his first public appearance in 1793. Making a tour of northern Italy in 1798, he was everywhere received with the utmost enthusiasm, despite his youthfulness, but fell a prey to dissipation. On one occasion, on the eve of a concert at Leghorn, having gambled away his money and pawned his violin, he had to borrow an instrument to keep his engagement. It was a Guarnerius, one of the finest in the world. After the concert, the owner of the violin declined to take it back, exclaiming, "Never will I profane the strings which your fingers have touched. That instrument is yours." Paganini used it at all his concerts, and bequeathed it to his native city, where it is still preserved in the museum. Among his many triumphs was that at Vienna in 1828, when the gold medal of Saint Salvator was conferred upon him by the city authorities and the title of Count virtuoso by the Emperor. A triumphant tour of Europe followed. Paganini died in Nice.

❖ ❖ ❖

Paganini knew the value of time and made few, if any, false motions. Having once mastered the violin, his only playing was done before audiences, never in private practise. Furthermore, he played only his own music. To be a Paganini, aside from his musical genius, is to be self-confident, self-sufficient, self-made.

LORD BYRON

Born 1788—Died 1824 Volume V—Page 201

AN EMINENT ENGLISH ROMANTIC POET

"Throughout his life Byron was a man in revolt; and it was only a variation of the old passion for freedom that led him to Greece and to his grave. The personal bravery of the man was proven more than once in his life, and on the approach of death he was undismayed."—Hubbard

♣

GEORGE GORDON, sixth Lord Byron, was born in London, the only son of Captain John Byron of the Guards, and Catherine Gordon, a Scottish heiress. Byron early exhibited mysanthropic tendencies, induced perhaps by his lameness and by parental mistreatment. At ten he succeeded to the title and estates of his grand-uncle, William Lord Byron. In 1805 the embryo poet entered Trinity College, Cambridge and soon afterward published his first book, *Hours of Idleness*. It was mercilessly assailed in the *Edinburgh Review*, and the attack prompted him to reply anonymously with the satire *English Bards and Scotch Reviewers*. Following a period of travel, Byron published the first two cantos of *Childe Harold* (1812), with immense success, and was at once enrolled among the great poets of his country. In 1815 he made an unfortunate marriage with Anne Isabella Milbanke, who left him after the birth of their daughter, Augusta Ada (afterward Countess of Lovelace). His domestic life became notoriously complicated, especially his relations with the Countess Guiccioli and a Miss Clairmont. In 1823 Byron joined the Greek insurgents, becoming a leader in the struggle for independence, and died from exposure and fever at Missolonghi.

♣ ♣ ♣

Byron, who "awoke one morning and found himself famous," is an example of the man of letters who, being economically independent, can afford to flout public opinion, and in so doing wins fame and fortune. On occasion the world enjoys being flouted, provided it is done bravely and brilliantly.

ELIZABETH B. BROWNING

Born 1806—Died 1861

Volume II—Page 17

FOREMOST WOMAN POET OF THE NINETEENTH CENTURY

"The love of Robert Browning and Elizabeth Barrett (the greatest poetess of the age) is an instance of the Divine Passion. Take off thy shoes, for the place whereon thou standest is holy ground!"—Hubbard.

❖

ELIZABETH BARRETT BROWNING was born, according to uncertain authority, near the city of Durham, England. She died in Florence, Italy. As a young girl she displayed great precosity, eagerly reading books beyond the comprehension of most children, and when about eleven years old composed an "epic poem," *The Battle of Marathon.* In 1826 she published anonymously *An Essay on Mind and other Poems*, giving evidence of unusual powers. In 1835 the family took up a residence in London, where Miss Barrett established her reputation by *The Seraphim and Other Poems* (1838). A hemorrhage, added to the shock caused by the death, in 1840, of a favorite brother, left her an invalid for years, during which time, however, she wrote much of her best poetry contained in a volume published in 1844. A year later she met Robert Browning, whom she had mentioned in her poem *Lady Geraldine's Courtship*, and they were married in 1846, much against her father's wishes. Proceeding to Italy, they lived in Florence, and there in 1849 their son Robert Wiedemann Barrett, was born. In 1850 appeared a collected edition of Mrs. Browning's work, followed by *Casa Guidi Windows* (1851), *Aurora Leigh* (1856), *Poems Before Congress* (1860) and *Last Poems*, posthumously published in 1862. Her *Sonnets From the Portuguese*, written after her engagement to Browning, are unrivaled, of their kind, in the English language.

❖ ❖ ❖

Spending the best years of her life on a sickbed, during which time she wrote most of her greatest poetry, Elizabeth Barrett Browning, as Hubbard presents her in the Little Journey, is a rare example of optimism and will-power triumphing over discouragement and despair.

FELIX MENDELSSOHN

Born 1809—Died 1847 Volume XIV—Page 163

A GREAT ROMANTIC COMPOSER

"He was the most precocious musical genius that ever lived, excepting Mozart; and Goethe, who knew them both, declared that Mendelssohn's music bore the same relationship to Mozart's as the talk of a grown-up cultured person to the prattle of a child."—Hubbard.

❖

FELIX MENDELSSOHN-BARTHOLDY was born in Hamburg, Germany, of wealthy Jewish parentage. He was brought up in the Protestant faith. His first composition was written before he was twelve years of age. At eleven the boy met and captivated Goethe, not only with his musical accomplishments but by his modesty and gentility. Notwithstanding his musical bent, Felix was taken by his father to Paris in 1825 to have Cherubini pass on his talent. The verdict was favorable to a musical career for him. In 1827 his *Midsummer Night's Dream* overture was given an enthusiastic reception. One of his finest achievements, the first performance since Bach's death of the *Saint Matthew Passion,* took place in Berlin in 1829. In that year he made a triumphal concert tour of the British Isles, the first of many visits to England. In 1830 he declined an offered professorship of music in the University of Berlin, and took up a residence in Italy. There he executed his great cantata to Goethe's *First Walpurgis Night* and the *Italian Symphony.* In 1833 he was made musical director of Düsseldorf, where his oratorio of Saint *Paul* was brought out under his own direction in 1836. The year following he married the daughter of a French minister in Frankfort. While in England in 1846 Mendelssohn brought out his oratorio *Elijah,* and died shortly after his return to Germany.

That inherited wealth and a luxurious upbringing do not necessarily stifle the incentive to do useful work in the world, is made plain in the Little Journey to the Home of Mendelssohn. No struggle for recognition marked his growth. Mendelssohn was what Hubbard calls "a born success," such as has no need of adversity to develop greatness.

FREDERIC CHOPIN

Born 1809—Died 1849 Volume XIV—Page 77

THE GREATEST MODERN MASTER OF PIANOFORTE COMPOSITION

"*Chopin wrote no lengthy symphonies, oratorios or operas. His music is poetry set to exquisite sounds. Poetry is an ecstacy of the spirit, and ecstacies in their very nature are not sustained moods. A composition by Chopin is a soul-ecstacy, like unto the singing of a lark.*"—Hubbard.

❖

FREDERIC FRANÇOIS CHOPIN was born at Zelazowa Wola, near Warsaw, Poland. His father was a professor in the Warsaw gymnasium, and the family was in comfortable circumstances. He received excellent instruction, and at twenty was an accomplished pianist. His first concert in Warsaw was given in 1830, and was followed by a second, the net receipts of both being $600, a considerable sum for a young pianist in those days. While giving concerts in Munich, in 1831, Chopin heard of the Russian occupation of Warsaw. Thus exiled he settled in Paris, which was his home for the remaining eighteen years of his life. Among his friends were Liszt, Heine, Berlioz, Mérimée, Meyerbeer, Balzac, Dumas, De Musset, Ary Scheffer and George Sand, with the last of whom he had a famous liaison. Several of his Etudes date from this period, among them the great C minor, Op. 10 No. 12, sometimes called the *Revolutionary*, because inspired by his wrath at the fall of Warsaw. In 1835 Chopin visited Germany and became engaged to the sister of two of his Polish schoolmates. The engagement was broken in 1837, the year he met George Sand. In that year he made a trip to England, where he developed tuberculosis. Following a second visit to England, in 1848, Chopin returned to Paris to die.

Chopin knew his limitations, and, knowing them, did not waste time or energy in trying to do things that were beyond him. By confining himself to the piano he made that instrument give up every secret it possessed, the result being that, although he worked in miniature, he ranks among the great composers.

ALFRED TENNYSON

Born 1809—Died 1892 Volume V—Page 69

THE MOST REPRESENTATIVE ENGLISH POET OF THE NINETEENTH CENTURY

"*Tennyson is always serene, sane and safe—his lines breathe purity and excellence. He is the poet of religion, of the home and fireside, of established order, of truth, justice and mercy as embodied in law.*"—Hubbard.

❖

ALFRED, FIRST BARON, TENNYSON was born at Somersby, in Lincolnshire, England, a village of which his father was rector. Going to Trinity College, Cambridge, in 1828, he was associated with a remarkable group of young men including Thackeray, Spedding, Trench, Monckton Milnes, afterwards Lord Houghton, Merivale, Alford and Arthur Henry Hallam, son of the historian, who discerned his friend's genius and in 1829 told Gladstone that Tennyson "promised fair to be the greatest poet of our generation, perhaps of our century." He left Cambridge without a degree in 1831, and two years later published a volume *Poems*, which contained many of his choicest minor pieces, *The Lady of Shallott, The Palace of Art, The Lotus-Eaters* and *A Dream of Fair Women.* It attracted no particular attention. Nine years passed before he made his place in English poetry secure with *Poems* in two volumes, in which were the first of the *Idylls of the King, Ulysses, Locksley Hall, Godiva, Break, Break, Break* and *The Two Voices.* In 1845 the Government granted him a pension of £200. In 1850 appeared his *In Memoriam,* a tribute to the memory of Arthur Hallam, in the same year he married Emily Sarah Sellwood, and was appointed poet laureate in succession to Wordsworth. In 1884 Tennyson was elevated to the peerage, and at his death he was buried in Westminster Abbey.

❖ ❖ ❖

Tennyson never wanted or tried to be anything but a poet. His singleness of purpose is the trait most clearly evident in the Little Journey to the great Victorian poet laureate of England.

ROBERT SCHUMANN

Born 1810—Died 1856 Volume XIV—Page 109

A FAMOUS GERMAN COMPOSER

"*Wherever hearts are sad, or glad, and songs are sung, and strings vibrate, and keys respond to love's caress, there is in hearts that know and feel, a shrine; and on this shrine in letters of gold two words are carved, and they are these: The Schumanns.*"—Hubbard.

❖

ROBERT SCHUMANN was born at Zwickau, Saxony. Until he was of age he had no instruction in musical composition, though he took lessons in piano playing while a student at the University of Leipzig. His instructor was Frederick Wieck, a gifted musician, whose daughter, Clara, was later to become Schumann's wife, inspiration and best interpreter. An accident for which Schumann himself was responsible forced him to give up piano playing and devote himself wholly to composition. Dissatisfied with the progress he was making as a pianist, he devised a system of digital gymnastics which so injured the sinews of the third finger of his right hand that he never fully regained its use. In 1831 he became a music critic for the *Allgemeine Musik-Zeitung*, and three years later he helped establish the *Neue Zeitschrift für Musick*, to wage war against philistinism in music. In 1840 Schumann married, much against the wishes of his wife's parents. His years of courtship were productive of some of his finest music. When Mendelssohn founded the conservatory at Leipzig, Schumann became one of the instructors. He resigned in 1844, and for the next six years lived in Dresden, where his *C major Symphony*, the opera *Genoveva*, the *Manfred* music and scenes from *Faust* were written. In 1854 he tried to drown himself, but was rescued and placed in a private asylum near Bonn, where he died.

❖ ❖ ❖

To turn an apparent misfortune—the injury of one of his fingers—to one's advantage is a point of interest brought out in the Little Journey to the Home of Schumann, the most "intimate" of composers and chief advocate of the Neo-Romantic School.

FRANZ LISZT

Born 1811—Died 1866 Volume XIV—Page 187

A GREAT HUNGARIAN PIANIST-COMPOSER

"In writing of Liszt there is a strong temptation to work the superlative to its limit. In this instance it is well to overcome the temptation by succumbing to it. . . . No finespun theory of pedagogics or heredity can account for the talent of Franz Liszt—he was one sent by God."—Hubbard.

❖

FRANZ LISZT was born at Raiding, Hungary, and died at Bayreuth, Bavaria. He made his first public appearance when only nine years old at Ödenburg. In 1823 at a concert in Vienna he received an ovation, and Beethoven kissed him after he had finished playing. He went to Paris to study, and became intimate with Victor Hugo, Lamartine, George Sand and other celebrities. His first operetta, *Don Sancho ou le château de l'amour*, was produced in 1825. Contemporary critics described him as "a pianist, the most extraordinary and fascinating ever known, and one of the most wonderful improvisators." Turning to teaching, he met with immediate success, aristocratic patrons and friends of his boyhood rallying to him, and enabling him to satisfy every social as well as musical ambition. From 1834 to 1844 lasted his connection with the Comtesse d'Agoult (Daniel Stern). They had three children, one of whom married Hans von Bülow and afterward Richard Wagner, of whom her father was a mighty champion. In 1849 Liszt became musical director at Weimar, where he brought out Wagner's *Tannhäuser* and *Lohengrin*, and Berlioz's *Benvenuto Cellini*. He resigned the position in 1861 and divided his time between Weimar, Rome and Budapest. In 1879 he received the tonsure, and is known as the Abbé Liszt.

❖ ❖ ❖

Not only was Liszt a great musician himself—never being excelled as a pianist—but he went out of his way to make other musicians, such as Wagner and Berlioz, famous, great. His generosity was as rare as his genius, in which Hubbard detects something akin to divinity. Liszt was too big and busy to be jealous.

Robert Browning

Born 1812—Died 1889 Volume V—Page 39

A Great English Poet-Philosopher

"Thrice blest was Browning, in that Fate allowed him to live his philosophy—to work his poetry up into life, and then again to transmute life and love into art. Success came his way so slowly that he was never subjected to the fierce, dazzling searchlight of publicity."—Hubbard.

❖

ROBERT BROWNING was born in Camberwell, a suburb of London. His father was a scholarly clerk in the Bank of England, and his mother the daughter of a German shipowner who had settled at Dundee, Scotland. In 1833 his first book, *Pauline*, was published anonymously, and two years later he published a metaphysical drama, entitled *Paracelsus*, which secured for Browning the friendship of Macready the actor, to whom he dedicated *Strafford* (1837), followed by *Sordello* (1840). During the next five years appeared periodically a series of poems bearing the collective title *Bells and Pomegranates*, and beginning with *Pippa Passes*, which received warm praise from Miss Barrett, whom he married in 1846. Most of their married life was spent in Italy, where much of Browning's greatest work was done and where his wife died in 1861. Thereafter Browning lived in England. His creative powers remained unimpaired to the end of his industrious life, the poem *Asolando* being published in London the day that Browning died in Venice. He was buried in Westminster Abbey. The Browning Society, established in London, in 1881, and similar organizations throughout England and the United States have by their discussions and publications done much to advance the study of his works.

His refusal to be discouraged in spite of the fact that he was well on toward middle age before his work received any general recognition, is a Browning characteristic upon which Hubbard lays emphasis. Browning exemplifies the necessity of having faith in oneself in order to accomplish any difficult undertaking.

RICHARD WAGNER

Born 1813—Died 1883 Volume XIV—Page 11

ORIGINATOR OF THE MUSIC-DRAMA

"*Wagner's unhappy marriage forms the keynote of his art. Every opera he wrote depicts a soul in bonds. From 'The Flying Dutchman' to 'Parsifal' we are shown the struggle of a strong man with cruel Fate; a reaching out for liberty and light; the halting between duty and inclination.*" —Hubbard.

❖

RICHARD WAGNER was born at Leipzig, Germany. He aimed at the colossal even as a boy, writing a tragedy at fourteen which he described as a jumble of *Hamlet* and *Lear*. It was to compose music for this tragedy that, in 1830, he entered the University of Leipzig. In 1833 he became a professional musician, occupying the post of chorus master at Würzburg. He became successively a conductor at Magdeburg, Königsburg and Riga, and added to his financial burdens, already critically heavy, by marrying, in 1836, Minna Planer, an actress in Königsburg. Subsequent to a visit to London, Wagner and his wife passed a trying period in Paris, where he composed and sold to the Paris Opera his *Flying Dutchman* sketches, which he later made into the opera first produced at Dresden in 1843. *Tannhäuser*, produced at Dresden in 1845, proved a greater puzzle to the public than *The Flying Dutchman.* Liszt, however, brought it out successfully at Weimar in 1848, an achievement which led to the now historic Wagner-Liszt friendship. *Lohengrin*, finished in 1848, also was brought out by Liszt. Tribulations followed, notably the famous Paris fiasco of *Tannhäuser* in 1861. After four years of widowerhood, in 1870 Wagner married Cosima von Bülow, a daughter of Liszt. In 1876 *The Ring of the Nibelung* was performed at Beyreuth, followed by *Parsifal* in 1882. Wagner died of heart disease in Venice.

Hubbard makes a Little Journey to Wagner as a great composer who "could have made his mark had he turned his attention to any other profession, or any branch of art or science." At the same time, Wagner is an illustration of the penalty one pays for exercising the fullest liberty or expression, regardless of who may be affected.

GIUSEPPE VERDI

Born 1813—Died 1901 Volume XIV—Page 275

GREATEST OF MODERN ITALIAN COMPOSERS

"There were no sad, solemn, recurring themes in the full-ripened fruit of Verdi's genius. When he died, at the age of eighty-seven, the curtain fell on the career of a great and potent personality—the one unique singer of the Nineteenth Century."—Hubbard.

❖

GIUSEPPE VERDI was born at Roncole, in the duchy of Parma, Italy. His first music instructor was the organist of the village church. Later he found a patron in the president of the Philharmonic Society at Busseto, whose conductor instructed him in composition and orchestration. At sixteen he sought to enter the conservatory at Milan, but was rejected for lack of musical ability. Nothing daunted, the future composer of *Aida*, *Rigoletto* and *Il Trovatore* applied to the conductor of La Scala, and in the course of time produced his first opera, *Oberto, Conte di San Bonifacio,* for the score of which he received 2,000 lire. He was guaranteed 4,000 lire for each of three operas to be written at intervals of eight months. As Hubbard recites, Verdi next collaborated with Merelli on the unsuccessful opera *Un Giorno di Regno*, and then, two years later (1842) scored a triumph with *Nabucodonosor*. In the following year *I Lombardi* appeared, and thereafter Verdi was regarded as the foremost composer of Italy. In 1844 *Ernani* was produced auspiciously in Venice. Following the production of *Rigoletto* (1851) and *Il Trovatore* and *La Traviata* (1853) his supremacy was unquestioned. *Otello* (1887) and *Falstaff* (1893) constituted his valedictory.

❖ ❖ ❖

Verdi was a businessman, as well as artist, and as Hubbard observes in the Little Journey to the Italian music master, he succeeded in getting the most for the mintage of his mind. Money fairly flowed his way. But the more money he was offered, the fewer and better were the operas he gave to the world. Verdi is an example to all artists.

WALT WHITMAN

Born 1819—Died 1892 Volume I—Page 163

A GREAT AMERICAN POET-PROPHET

"*Whitman sings the beauty and the glory of the present. He rebukes our groans and sighs—bids us look about on every side at the wonders of creation, and at the miracles within our grasp. He lifts us up . . . infuses into us courage, manly pride, self-reliance.*"—Hubbard.

❖

WALT (ORIGINALLY WALTER) WHITMAN, regarded by many as the most significant, if not the greatest, of American poets, was born at West Hills (now Huntington) Long Island. While in his twenties he edited the Brooklyn *Eagle* for a year, making contacts which did much toward shaping his philosophy. His first and chief work, *Leaves of Grass*, was published in 1855. It was received with mingled abuse and amusement, and did not begin to have a general audience until Emerson gave it a glowing appraisal. On first reading the book, Emerson records that he rubbed his eyes a little "to see if this sunbeam were no illusion." He wrote Whitman: "I find it the most extraordinary piece of wit and wisdom that America has yet contributed. I am very happy in reading it. I find incomparable things said incomparably well. I greet you at the beginning of a great career." During the Civil War, Whitman was a volunteer army nurse. One result of this experience was *Drum-Taps* (1865) subsequently included in *Leaves of Grass*. After the war he held a Government clerkship at Washington, but suffered a stroke of paralysis in 1873. Subsequently he resided at Camden, New Jersey, the home of his brother George, and remained there until his death. His grave is in Camden.

❖ ❖ ❖

On cannot take the Little Journey with Hubbard to the Home of Walt Whitman without becoming more of an individualist. Be yourself! Stand on your own feet! is the way Hubbard would put it. Appositely, the founder and conductor of the Roycroft Shops was himself one of the greatest individualists of his generation.

CHRISTINA ROSSETTI

Born 1830—Died 1894 Volume II—Page 115

A DISTINGUISHED WOMAN POET

"Christina Rossetti comes to us as one of those splendid stars that are so far away they are seen only at rare intervals. . . . She had the faculty of seizing beautiful moments, exalted feelings, sublime emotions, and working them up into song that comes echoing to us as from across soft seas."—Hubbard.

❖

CHRISTINA GEORGINA ROSSETTI, sister of Dante Gabriel Rossetti, was born in London, England. She was brought up entirely at home under her mother's tuition, as a member of the Anglican Church. She began writing verse in early girlhood. Before she was seventeen a volume of her poetry was privately printed by her maternal grandfather, who kept a printing press for his own convenience at his residence in London. Her publications are *Goblin-Market and Other Poems* (1862), *The Prince's Progress and Other Poems* (1866), *Singsong* (1872), *A Pageant and Other Poems* (1881); and in prose, *Commonplace and Other Stories, Speaking Likenesses* and a few devotional volumes. Most of her poems were reissued in 1890; and after her death, her brother William edited a complete edition of her works. She lived a very secluded life, divided between devoted attention to her grandparents and her mother (who died at an advanced age in 1886), and earnest religious thought and practice. In direct poetic gift and intrinsic quality of poetry she may be regarded as equal to her brother Dante Gabriel, although her poetry is of a less conspicuous kind. She is at her best in short and intense lyrics such as *After Death* and *Passing and Glassing.* As a poet her only equal among the English women of the nineteenth century was Elizabeth Barrett Browning.

❖ ❖ ❖

Christina Rossetti found time to write imperishable poetry during intervals in a lifetime devoted to housework, caring for elderly kinfolk and nursing a mentally afflicted brother. She is an example to those who have a tendency to neglect or ignore commonplace duties and responsibilities in their ambition to express themselves in art.

JOHANNES BRAHMS

Born 1833—Died 1897 Volume XIV—Page 333

A NOTED GERMAN COMPOSER OF CHORAL AND CHAMBER MUSIC

"Brahms knew the world—not simply one little part of it—he knew it as thoroughly as any man can, and was interested in it all. He knew the world of workers—the toilers and bearers of burdens. He knew the weak and the vicious, and his heart went out to them in sympathy."—Hubbard.

❖

JOHANNES BRAHMS was born in Hamburg and died in Vienna. His debut was made at the age of fourteen, when he played a set of his own variations. In 1853, in the course of a concert tour, he was "discovered" by Schumann, who published a glowing tribute to the young musician. In 1854 he became conductor for the Prince of Lippe-Detmold. From 1858 to 1862 he was in Hamburg and Switzerland, pursuing further musical studies. In 1862 he was in Vienna, where, in 1863-4, he conducted the Singakademie. He lived in various places, including Baden-Baden, until 1869, when he again went to Vienna. From 1871 to 1874 he was conductor of the Gesellschaft der Musikfreunde. Afterwards he lived near Heidelberg until 1878, when he permanently settled in Vienna. To an offer of the degree of Mus. Doc. from Cambridge University, England, he paid no attention in 1877, but in 1881 he accepted a Ph. D. from Breslau. Brahms composed nearly a hundred and sixty songs besides his symphonies, but no operas. His service to art consists in his having created, within established forms, music original, modern and beautiful. The great work which established his reputation in Germany was his *German Requiem.*

❖ ❖ ❖

To Brahms a Little Journey is made as a man with a rare and remarkable genius for music composition, who, at the same time, was as much, if not more, interested in a dozen other forms of occupation. It might almost be said that the work which immortalized Brahms was a side-issue.

BOOK SEVEN

❖

PHILOSOPHY AND RELIGION

MOSES

Born 1571 B.C.—Died 1451 B.C. Volume X—Page 11

FOUNDER AND LAW-GIVER OF ISRAEL

"*Moses was the first man in history who fought for human rights and sought to make men free, even from their own limitations. . . . The laws of Moses were designed for the Now and Here. Many of them ring true and correct even today, after all this interval of more than three thousand years.*"—Hubbard.

❖

MOSES was born in Egypt, and for three months after that event was kept concealed by his mother to evade the command of Pharaoh that all male Hebrew children be drowned in the Nile. According to Biblical record, he was then exposed in a box among the rushes on the river bank, and was found by an Egyptian princess, who adopted and reared him. After he had grown up he one day slew an Egyptian whom he saw maltreating a Hebrew slave. Fearing punishment, he fled into the desert and found asylum in an oasis inhabited by the Kenites. There he married Zipporah, daughter of a priest of Midian, and tended the flocks of his father-in-law. While thus occupied the prophetic spirit came upon him and he returned to Egypt for the purpose of delivering his brethren from bondage. A series of plagues was attributed by Pharoah to the God of Moses, and the Hebrews were ordered out of Egypt. Moses was their leader during forty years of "wandering in the wilderness," which period he utilized for perfecting a civil organization and for preparing a code of laws of a high ethical, religious, sanitary and political character. Jewish tradition ascribes to him the authorship of the Pentateuch, with the exception of the verses describing his death.

❖ ❖ ❖

Moses, besides being the law-giver of the Israelites, was, as Hubbard enumerates, a soldier, a diplomat, an executive, a writer, a teacher, a prophet, a stonecutter, a farmer and shepherd. To lead a host of people out of the darkness of slavery into the light of freedom, as Moses did, requires extraordinary talent and ability not only in one but in many directions.

PYTHAGORAS

Born about 582 B. C.—Died about 500 B. C. Volume X—Page 71

A FAMOUS GREEK PHILOSOPHER

"*Pythagoras was one of those strange beings who are born with a desire to know, and who finally comprehending the secret of the Sphinx, that there is really nothing to say, insist on saying it.*"—Hubbard.

❖

PYTHAGORAS was born in Samos, Greece, and died at Metapontum, Magna Græcia. He had become known in Ionia as a man of great learning when, perhaps driven from home by disgust at the tyranny of Polycrates about 530 B.C., he migrated to Magna Græcia and settled at Crotona. There he founded an exclusive brotherhood which became involved in the fierce struggles between the aristocracy and democracy that were at the time raging in lower Italy; and when the popular party gained the upper hand it turned furiously upon the Pythagorean brothers and burned them in their meeting places. Only a few escaped. Pythagoras is said to have traveled from Persia to Gaul in search of wisdom, to have become initiated in Egypt into the venerable mysteries of that country, and there to have acquired mathematical lore and a belief in the transmigration of souls. He is credited with all sorts of miraculous performances, such as appearing in two places simultaneously, exhibiting to the assembled spectators at Olympia his thigh of gold, and taming wild beasts at a word of command. All this testifies to the wonder excited among his disciples by his superior knowledge and to the religious veneration in which he was held by them. Pythagoras himself wrote nothing, and every disciple strove to gain credit for his own phase of Pythagoreanism by attributing it to the venerated master.

❖ ❖ ❖

Pythagoras, to whom Hubbard devotes a Little Journey as "the wisest as well as the most learned man of his time," resorted to tricks of legerdemain to impress his really beneficent teachings upon his disciples, thereby anticipating the assertion of the great modern showman, Barnum, that the majority of people like to be humbugged.

CONFUCIUS

Born 551 B.C.—Died 478 B.C. Volume X—Page 43

THE GREAT CHINESE PHILOSOPHER

Confucius was simply a teacher, and what he taught was the science of living. . . . He is the first man in point of time to proclaim the divinity of service, the brotherhood of man, and the truth that in useful work there is no high nor low degree."—Hubbard.

❖

CONFUCIUS, the most famous of all the sages of China, was of a military family akin to the ancient nobility, his father being governor-general of the District of Chow. When Confucius was three years of age he lost his father, but the boy was most carefully educated by his mother and trained according to the highest Chinese ideals. At seventeen he was manager for a wealthy landowner of Lu, and two years later he married. As in the case of other great teachers, however, notably Buddha, and later, Rama Krishna of India, Confucius seems to have been little adapted for family life. He had one son and, it would seem, two daughters during his four years of married life. From the age of twenty-two he devoted himself to teaching, and thence on for fifty-one years he migrated periodically from place to place. By the age of thirty he had formulated the tenets of his philosophy. In 517 B. C. he gained his first pupils of importance and coincidentally met Laotze, the founder of Taoism. There followed a period of some fifteen years of teaching in his native State of Lu, when his growing fame brought about his appointment to the governorship of Chung-tu, and other even higher honors. Subsequently he became a confirmed nomad and did not return to Lu until 485, seven years before his death. Confucius was, in his own words, not a reformer but a conserver.

❖ ❖ ❖

Confucius admonished the humblest of his disciples and followers to grow and develop—to be the superior men that they were capable of becoming. His encouraging doctrine is that each of us is born with resources that will enable their possessor to keep on developing to the end of his days.

SOCRATES

Born 469 B. C.—Died 399 B. C. Volume VIII—Page 11

FIRST OF ATHENIAN PHILOSOPHERS

"If Socrates ever came to know himself, he knew this fact: as an economic unit he was an absolute failure; but as a gadfly, stinging men into thinking for themselves, he was a success. A specialist is a deformity contrived by Nature to get the work done."—Hubbard.

❖

SOCRATES was born and died in Athens. His father was a sculptor and his mother a midwife. He at first adopted sculpture as his life work: in the time of Pausanias a group of draped Graces by him stood on the approach to the Acropolis. He soon, however, devoted himself entirely to the pursuit of philosophy, and became famous through the persistency and skill with which, in conversation with the sophists and with everyone who would submit themselves to his peculiar style of interrogation, he conducted the analysis of philosophical and ethical ideas. He was preeminently a searcher after a knowledge of virtue, and was in himself the noblest exponent of the ethical life of the Greeks. He rendered conspicuous military service at Potidæa (431 B. C.), Delium (424 B. C.) and Amphipolis (422 B. C.); and opposed the Thirty Tyrants at the risk of his life and liberty. He is the chief character in the dialogues of Plato, in which his teachings are set forth, and is the subject of the *Memorabilia* of Xenophon. His most famous pupils were Plato, Xenophon and Alcibiades. He was bitterly attacked by Aristophanes as a sophist and innovator, and made many enemies by his mode of life and the character of his opinions. In 399 B. C. he was accused of impiety (the introduction of new gods) and of corrupting the youth; defended himself in a famous speech in defiance of his judges; was condemned, and drank hemlock in prison, surrounded by his disciples.

❖ ❖ ❖

Hubbard makes the Little Journey to Socrates as a pioneer in undertaking to get acquainted with himself rather than to waste his time on the outside world. The self-control which he exemplified and the self-knowledge which he inculcated are the keynotes of his philosophy.

PLATO

Born 427 B. C.—Died 347 B. C. Volume X—Page 99

FOUNDER OF THE ACADEMIC SCHOOL OF PHILOSOPHY

"*Plato was a teacher of teachers, and like every other great teacher who has ever lived, his soul goes marching on, for to teach is to influence, and influence never dies. Hail Plato!*"—Hubbard.

❖

PLATO, so surnamed from his broad shoulders, his real name being Aristocles, was born at Ægina and died at Athens. He was a disciple of Socrates and a teacher of Aristotle. His parents were of the Greek aristocracy, and in his youth Plato was a successful gymnast, a soldier and a poet. After he became a disciple of Socrates he is said to have destroyed his poems, but some epigrams attributed to him are extant. His association with Socrates dated from an early age until the latter died. After this event he went to Eucleides at Megara, and later sojourned in Egypt, Cyrene, Sicily and Magna Græcia. By Dionysius of Syracuse, who was offended at his opinions, Plato was delivered to the Spartan ambassador Pollis, who sold him as a slave in Ægina. He was ransomed, returned to Athens and founded The Academy, the school so called from the public playground near Athens which once was the property of the military hero Academus. In 367 B. C. and 361 B. C. Plato revisited Syracuse on the invitation of Dion and Dionysius the Younger. He then returned to Athens, where he lived until his death, which occurred at a marriage-feast. All his genuine works have been preserved. They include the dialogues *Protagoras, Phædrus, Symposium, Gorgias, Republic, Sophist, Politicus* and *Laws*.

❖ ❖ ❖

As far back as the time of Alexander the Great it seemed desirable to a rich man's son, Plato, to become an ill-paid philosopher, to go to jail and suffer exile rather than to enjoy his inheritance. Plato is pictured in the Little Journey as one who regarded the life of thought, of contemplation, infinitely superior to the life of action.

ARISTOTLE

Born 384 B. C.—Died 322 B. C. Volume VIII—Page 83

FOUNDER OF THE PERIPATETIC SCHOOL OF PHILOSOPHY

"*In morals the world has added nothing new to the philosophy of Aristotle: gentleness, consideration, moderation, mutual helpfulness, and the principle that one man's privileges end where another man's rights begin —these make up the sum.*"—Hubbard.

❖

ARISTOTLE was born at Stagira, in Chalcidice, and died at Chalcis, in Eubœa. He was the son of Nicomachus, physician and friend of Amyntas, king of Macedonia. In his eighteenth year he went to Athens and became a pupil of Plato, with whom he remained for twenty years. Following the death of Plato, about 343 B. C., he was called to the court of Philip of Macedon to undertake the education of his son Alexander (afterward "the Great"), then thirteen years old. In 335 he returned to Athens where he established his school of philosophy and produced the greater part of his scientific works. He taught in the Lyceum. On the death of Alexander the uprising against the Macedonians forced Aristotle to flee from Athens (323 B. C.) to Chalcis, as he said, to save the Athenians from a second sin against philosophy, the first having been the enforced suicide of Socrates. There he died in his sixty-third year. Aristotle left behind him an enormous number of writings. Diogenes Laërtius, of uncertain date, gives a list of forty-six works dealing with all the then known branches of science. They fall into four groups: the logical, the metaphysical, and those relating to natural science, the ethical and the *Poetics* and *Rhetoric*. Aristotle's influence upon the development of philosophy and science has been enormous and continues to the present day.

❖ ❖ ❖

That greatness, even in the field of philosophy, provokes envy and is dangerous, is made evident in the Little Journey to Aristotle, who died in humiliating exile after being forced to flee from Athens. As Hubbard says, "Athens had none to match him; his very greatness was his offense."

SENECA

Born 4 B. C.—Died 65 A. D. Volume VIII—Page 45

A CELEBRATED ROMAN STOIC PHILOSOPHER

"Seneca was one of the purest and loftiest intellects the world has ever known. . . . Every ethical maxim of Christianity was expressed by this 'noble pagan,' and his influence was always directed toward that which he thought was right."—Hubbard.

❖

LUCIUS ANNÆUS SENECA was born at Corduba and died at his villa near Rome. When a child he accompanied his parents to Rome, where he studied rhetoric and philosophy and rose to prominence in what would now be called the legal profession. He was a senator under Caligula. Subsequently, in the reign of the Emperor Claudius (41 A. D.) he was banished to Corsica at the instigation of the Empress Messalina, who accused him of improper intimacy with Julia, the daughter of Germanicus. He was recalled in 49 A. D. through the influence of Agrippina, the new wife of Claudius, who intrusted him with the education of her son Nero. On the accession of his pupil in 54 A. D. he obtained virtual control of the government, which he exercised in concert with the prætorian prefect Burrus. The restraint which his counsel imposed on the emperor made his tenure of power precarious, and on the assassination of Burrus in 62 A. D. he sought permission to retire from the court. Through the imperial bounty his accumulated wealth amounted to 300,000 sestertia, or about $12,000,000. He was ultimately charged with complicity in the conspiracy of Piso, and took his own life in obedience to the order of Nero. Seneca wrote voluminously on moral subjects, and was the author of a number of tragedies which greatly influenced the Renaissance and French classical drama.

❖ ❖ ❖

Seneca is the first philosopher on record to become a multimillionaire. The Little Journey devoted to him shows that it is not inconsistent for a philosopher to enjoy the material benefits and luxuries of life, provided it does not result in a deterioration of character.

MARCUS AURELIUS

Born 121—Died 180 Volume VIII—Page 113

AN IMPERIAL PHILOSOPHER

"*Marcus Aurelius, the wise judge, saw that most litigation is foolish and absurd—both parties are at fault, and both are right. And to bring about the good time when men shall live in peace he began earnestly to govern himself. His ideal was a state where men would need no governing.*"—Hubbard.

❖

MARCUS AURELIUS, surnamed, Antoninus, was born in Rome. At seventeen he was adopted by the Emperor Antoninus Pius, successor to Hadrian; and Faustina, daughter of Antoninus, was selected for his wife. In the year 140 he was made consul, and in 161 became emperor, with Lucius Verus, also an adopted son of Antoninus Pius, as his associate in the government. He was a pupil of the Stoic Cornelius Fronto, and is frequently called "the philosopher" on account of his devotion to philosophy and literature. In 162 Verus undertook an expedition against the Parthians, but soon abandoned himself to dissipation at Antioch. His generals, however, were victorious, subduing Mesopotamia and enabling him to dictate terms of peace in 165. Verus died in 169, leaving his colleague sole emperor. Although fond of peace, both from natural disposition and philosophic culture, Marcus Aurelius displayed the sternest rigor in suppressing the revolts of the barbarians; but to do so he had to enlist vast numbers of gladiators and slaves, for his army had been thinned by a plague. In 175 the general Avidius Cassius organized a revolt in Syria, but was assassinated by his own officers. The conduct of Marcus Aurelius on hearing of his enemy's death attested his sublimity of character. He died either at Vienna or Sirmium. He wrote in Greek *The Meditations of Marcus Aurelius.*

❖ ❖ ❖

Marcus Aurelius is a signal example of a man in possession of unlimited power, who yet practices moderation in all his acts, strives to be just and develops a philosophic mind. His success in so doing has made him, as Hubbard states, "a guiding star—an inspiration—to untold millions."

HYPATIA

Born 370—Died 430 Volume X—Page 271

FIRST OF WOMEN PHILOSOPHERS

"She was the Ralph Waldo Emerson of her day. Her philosophy was Transcendentalism. In fact, she might be spoken of as the original charter member of the Concord School of Philosophy. Her theme was the New Thought, for New Thought is the oldest form of thought of which we know."—Hubbard.

❖

HYPATIA was born in Alexandria, Egypt, the daughter of Theon, whose celebrity as an astronomer and mathematician is obscured by that of his daughter. Her sex, youth, beauty and harsh fate have made her the most interesting martyr of philosophy. After receiving instruction in mathematics from her father, who was a professor at the Museum in Alexandria, she succeeded him as a lecturer, Her growing fame drew students from all parts of the East, where the influence of Greek thought and knowledge was felt. Egypt was proud of her, and such reliance was placed upon her judgment and sagacity that Alexandria magistrates were accustomed to consult her on important cases. Among her intimates was Orestes, prefect of the city. Her influence over him excited the jealousy and hatred of the Archbishop Cyril, who found no difficulty in directing the brutal violence of a superstitious mob against one who was described as an enemy of the faith and its ministers. Headed by an ecclesiastic named Peter, a band of fanatics attacked Hypatia in the spring of 415 A. D., as she was passing through the streets in her chariot, dragged her to one of the churches, where they stripped and then murdered her, tearing her body to pieces and committing her mutilated remains to the flames.

❖ ❖ ❖

Hubbard takes us on a Little Journey to Hypatia, now dead some fifteen hundred years, to show that women are not necessarily of inferior intellect to men and never have been. Where there was one Hypatia in the fourth and fifth centuries, her many successors are constantly growing in numbers, advantages and influence.

SAINT BENEDICT

Born 480—Died 543 Volume X—Page 295

FOUNDER OF THE ORDER OF BENEDICTINES

"*The Book of Rules by Benedict . . . reveals an insight that will appeal to all who have had to do with socialistic experiments, not to mention the management of labor unions. Benedict was one of the industrial leaders of the world. His life was an epoch, and his influence still abides.*"—Hubbard.

❖

SAINT BENEDICT was born at Nursia, in Umbria, Italy. At an early age he was sent to the schools of literature and jurisprudence in Rome, but soon grew dissatisfied with the character of instruction. Resolving to lead a religious life, he left Rome and for three years dwelt in a cavern, which afterwards received the name Holy Grotto, until his fame spread over the country and multitudes came to see him. Wealthy Romans placed their sons in his charge, and he eventually founded twelve cloisters, over each of which he placed a superior. About 529 he established a monastery on Monte Cassino, which became one of the richest and most celebrated in Italy. There he had his famous interview with Totila, King of the Goths, whom he berated for his errors. In 515 Benedict is said to have composed his *Regula Monachorum*, in which he aimed, among other things, at repressing the irregular and licentious life of the wandering monks by introducing stricter discipline and order. These wise regulations dispensed with useless maceration, and divided the time of the monks into periods of prayer, mental and manual labor; they were obliged to till the soil, also to read and copy manuscripts. Some literary life was thus preserved in the monasteries, and the dependencies of the Order formed what are now called model farms.

❖ ❖ ❖

St. Benedict was one of the first great churchmen to preach the gospel of labor. Hubbard calls the founder of the religious order which bears his name "a great pioneer captain of industry, who had to fight inertia, selfishness and incipient paranoia, just as does the man who tries to introduce practical socialism today."

SAVONAROLA

Born 1452—Died 1498 Volume VII—Page 81

A Noted Italian Reformer

"He saw the wickedness of the world and sought to shun it by fleeing to a monastery. There he saw the wickedness of the monastery, and there being no place to flee he sought to purify it. And at the same time he sought to purify and better the world by standing outside of the world."
—Hubbard.

❖

GIROLAMO SAVONAROLA was born at Ferrara and was executed at Florence, Italy. He received a good education and entered the Dominican Order at Bologna in 1475. It was not until 1490, at the Monastery of San Marco in Florence, that he began to preach with such boldness and fervor as to attract general attention. His period of influence came just as the earlier inspiration of the Renaissance painters was dying out, just as the great Cinquecento period was dawning. His voice was raised loudly against the corrupting influences that were paganizing art. Among his devoted disciples were Botticelli and Fra Bartolommeo, who abandoned their art to follow him. Lorenzo the Magnificent, ruler of Florence, who died in 1492, had tried unsuccessfully to win over Savonarola, whose denunciations were openly directed at the reigning family. In a revolt that followed the invasion of Italy by Charles VIII of France, 1494, Piero di Medici was driven from Florence and the power of Savonarola became formidable. He aimed at establishing an ideal Christian commonwealth, and for a time Florence appeared to be a new city. His attack on Pope Alexander VI proved to be his undoing. He was forbidden to preach in 1495 and two years later he was excommunicated, although he declined to accept the Papal mandate and openly rebelled from the authority of the Pope. In 1498 Savonarola was imprisoned, tried for heresy and sedition, hanged and his body burned.

❖ ❖ ❖

As a religious reformer Savonarola made the mistake of setting his standard too high, of demanding such virtue and devotion from his followers that they found his teachings irksome, and eventually revolted and slew him. As Hubbard makes plain in the Little Journey to the severe Florentine zealot, a little less austerity and a little more common sense and diplomacy would have led him to triumph instead of disaster.

ERASMUS

Born 1466—Died 1536 Volume X—Page 151

A GREAT THEOLOGIAN OF THE RENAISSANCE

"Luther split the power of the Pope. Erasmus thought it a calamity to do so, because he believed that strife of sects tended to make men lose sight of the one essential in religion—harmony—and cause them simply to struggle for victory."—Hubbard.

❖

DESIDERIUS ERASMUS was born at Rotterdam, Holland. He received a good education, and was ordained for the priesthood, entering the service of the Bishop of Cambray in 1491. Under the patronage of that dignitary he was enabled to study at the University of Paris. He subsequently visited the chief European countries, including England (1498-99 and 1510-14), and in 1521 settled at Basel, whence he removed to Freiburg in 1529. In Basel he was the intimate of a circle of reforming scholars who gathered about the famous publisher John Froben. In Italy he was for a time a member of the household of the Venetian publisher Aldus Manutius. His correspondence, including more than 1,500 letters, shows him in relations with more than 500 persons, many of them of the highest station. Down to the year 1517, when the Lutheran revolt began, the work of Erasmus was largely in criticism of the existing Roman Catholic Church system and of the scholastic method in philosophy by which it was defended. In his *Manual or Dagger of the Christian Soldier* (1523) he emphasizes the uselessness of forms in religion, as compared to the spirit of sincere apostolic piety. He aimed to reform, without dismembering, the Roman Church. His chief work was an edition of the New Testament in Greek with a Latin translation, published in 1516.

❖ ❖ ❖

By failing to come into a fortune that was willed to him, Erasmus was enabled to develop into a great theologian. In the Little Journey to this eminent scholar of the Renaissance and Reformation period stress is laid upon the fact that apparent misfortune may be the thing most needful to a great eventual accomplishment.

MARTIN LUTHER

Born 1483—Died 1546 Volume VII—Page 111

"FOUNDER OF PROTESTANT CIVILIZATION"

"Luther was a 'sensational preacher,' and he was an honest preacher. . . . He thundered against thc profligacy of the rich, the selfishness of Society, the iniquities of the government, the excesses of the monks, the laxity of discipline in the schools, and the growing tendency to worship the Golden Calf."—Hubbard.

❖

MARTIN LUTHER was a native of Eisleben, Saxony, and came of peasant parentage. At eighteen he entered the university at Erfurt, and devoted himself mainly to philosophy, though he was intended for the law. Graduating in 1505, he determined to become a monk, and, against the wishes of his family, entered the Augustine monastery at Erfurt. Two years later he was consecrated a priest, and in 1508 was called as professor of philosophy to the University of Wittenberg. His first important action in the direction of ecclesiastical reform was his publication, in 1517, of 95 theses against the sale of indulgences by the Dominican Tetzel. He was charged with heresy, and in 1520 was excommunicated, following the publication of his famous *Address to the Christian Nobles of the German Nation.* He retaliated by publicly burning the bull of excommunication. At the Diet of Worms, 1521, whither he was summoned by the Emperor Charles V, he made the celebrated speech which ended with: "There I take my stand. I can do naught else. So help me God. Amen." Nevertheless, he was proscribed by the emperor. To escape the imperial wrath he lived in hiding for a time, during which he translated the New Testament into German, published in 1522. His translation of the whole Bible, completed in 1532, was published in 1534. Luther thereby became the founder of the present literary language of Germany. His complete works comprise 67 volumes.

❖ ❖ ❖

It was the distinction of Martin Luther to voice the growing liberality of religious opinion in his time. Hubbard makes a Little Journey to him, not as an innovator, but as a loyal churchman who wished to benefit the Church by freeing it from the faults that he feared would disintegrate it. That he was excommunicated was an indictment of a great body of Catholics for whom he spoke, and whose spiritual descendents are known as Lutherans.

JOHN KNOX

Born 1505—Died 1572 Volume IX—Page 187

THE GREAT SCOTTISH REFORMER

"Only a bold man, rough and coarse, could have defied the reigning powers and done the work which Destiny had cut out for John Knox to do. His power lay in the hallucination that his utterances were the final expressions of truth. Had he known more he would have done less."
—Hubbard.

❖

JOHN KNOX was born at Haddington and died at Edinburgh, Scotland. In 1522 he entered Glasgow University, but does not appear to have graduated. He studied law, and in 1544 became tutor to Alexander Cockburn, eldest son of the Laird of Ormiston. At this time George Wishart, sought asylum in the Cockburn home and exercised a powerful influence on Knox. In 1546 Wishart was burned at St. Andrews for heresy. His death was avenged by the murder of Cardinal Beaton soon afterward. In the following year Knox accepted a "call" from the congregation at St. Andrews, was imprisoned because of his teachings, was released, went to England and in 1551 was made one of the six royal chaplains. In 1554 he visted Calvin at Geneva, and for a while was pastor of the English congregation at Frankfort-on-the--Main. In 1556 he was summoned by the bishops to appear at Blackfriars Kirk in Edinburgh, but his following was so powerful that the prosecution was abandoned. Two years later he published his *Blasts of the Trumpet Against the Monstrous Regiment of Women*, directed against Mary of Guise, regent of Scotland, Queen Mary of England and Catharine de Medici. Following a turbulent career, marked by clashes with Mary Queen of Scots, and by his organization of the Presbyterian Church, his strength was exhausted and he died, as he said, "weary of the world."

❖ ❖ ❖

In the Little Journey to the leader of the Scotch Reformation Hubbard depicts a character distinguished by firmness and decision and a plain, severely harsh sense of reality. Here is a strong man of stern convictions, who feels no scruples and recognizes no dangers in carrying out his aims. The end justifies the means, to the John Knox type of man.

ANNE HUTCHINSON

Born 1590—Died 1643 Volume IX—Page 337

LEADER OF THE ANTINOMIAN SECT IN NEW ENGLAND

"*Man is not a finality—he is not the thing—the play's the thing: life is the play and the play is life. Man is only one of the properties. Look out, not in; up, not down, and lend a hand. And these things form the modern application of the philosophy of Anne Hutchinson.*"—Hubbard.

❖

ANNE (MARBURY) HUTCHINSON was born in Lincolnshire, England. With her husband and their fifteen children, she emigrated to Massachusetts in 1634. Living in a community prone to religious excitement, she held meetings for women in which she set forth the doctrine that those who were in the covenant of grace were not under the covenant of works, which was considered Antinomian by the State clergy and likely to have sad practical consequences. Great controversies arose, and a synod was called, in which her teachings were condemned and she was banished from the Colony. She went first to Rhode Island and with her followers founded the town of Portsmouth in 1638. The church in Boston, from which she had been excommunicated, vainly sent a deputation to Rhode Island with the hope of reclaiming her. After the death of her husband (who shared her opinions), in 1642, she removed with her surviving family to the Dutch settlement of New Amsterdam, now New York. The precise locality where she settled has been a matter of dispute, but according to the best authorities it was near Hell Gate, a stretch of water which separates Long Island from the mainland of New York. The Dutch and Indians were then at war, and in a savage onslaught her house was burned and herself and family, excepting one child who was taken captive, perished either in the flames or were slain.

To Anne Hutchinson a Little Journey is devoted as a religious leader who cheerfully braved death, persecution and banishment for the sake of her faith. Having escaped with her life from the zealous Puritan authorities of Massachusetts Colony, it was the irony of fate that she should be killed by Indians in a case of mistaken identity.

SPINOZA

Born 1632—Died 1677 Volume VIII—Page 201

THE GREATEST MODERN EXPOUNDER OF PANTHEISM

"His modesty, patience, kindness and freedom from all petty whim and prejudice set Spinoza apart as a marked man. Withal he was eminently religious, and the reference to him by Novalis as 'the God-intoxicated man' seems especially applicable to one who saw God in everything."—Hubbard.

❖

BARUCH, or BENEDICT, SPINOZA was born at Amsterdam, Holland. Of Hebrew parentage, he was carefully educated in Jewish theology and speculation. He was, however, alienated from the faith of his fathers by studies of physical science by the pantheistic writings of Descartes and Giordano Bruno. In 1656 he was condemned by the Jewish congregation of Amsterdam as a heretic, and excommunicated. From this time on he supported himself by grinding lenses, an art in which he was very proficient. He lived with a friend, who was in sympathy with his theological convictions, just outside of Amsterdam until early in 1661, when they removed to the village of Rhynsburg, near Leyden. In 1664 he went to Voorburg, a suburb of The Hague, and in 1670 took up his residence in The Hague itself. An attempt upon his life was made in Amsterdam in 1656. Previous to his expulsion from the Jewish community Spinoza is said to have fallen in love with the daughter of Van den Ende, his master in Greek and Latin, and to have had his suit rejected. The Elector Palatine, Charles Lewis, offered him a chair at the University of Heidelberg, which Spinoza declined as threatening to restrict his liberty of thinking. An offer of a pension, on condition of his dedicating a work to Louis XIV, he likewise rejected not long before his death.

❖ ❖ ❖

A Little Journey is devoted to Spinoza as a religious zealot, who antagonized his family and ignored all opportunities for worldly advancement that promised to interfere with his independence of thought and way of faith. Freedom to live and worship according to his own convictions, rather than the convictions of some one else, was to Spinoza the most important thing in the world.

MADAME GUYON

Born 1648—Died 1717 Volume II—Page 43

A DISTINGUISHED FRENCH RELIGIONIST

"The burden of her philosophy was 'Quietism'—the absolute submission of the human soul to the will of God. . . . She taught of power through repose, and told that you can never gain peace by striving for it like fury."—Hubbard.

❖

JEANNE MARIE BOUVIER DE LA MOTTE-GUYON was born at Montargis, and died at Blois, France. Her parents were of the nobility. In her girlhood she wished to enter a convent, but was prevailed upon when not quite sixteen to marry Jacques de la Motte-Guyon, son of a wealthy contractor who constructed the Canal of Briare, for which he was ennobled. In 1676 she was left a wealthy widow with five children, whose education she superintended for several years. About 1680, after settling most of her fortune on her children, she went to Geneva for religious work, and wrote a *Short and Easy Method of Prayer*, besides commentaries on the Scriptures, which brought her under ecclesiastical censure. She was accused of laying too much stress on faith and the quietude of contemplation rather than good works in the Christian life. Shut up by a royal order in the Convent of the Visitation (1688), she was liberated through the influence of Madame de Maintenon. Soon thereafter she found a champion in Fenelon, Archbishop of Cambray, who was convinced of her uprightness and good intentions. (See Volume XIII—Fenelon and Madame Guyon). Politics became a factor in her condemnation and in her imprisonment in the Bastile in 1700. She was released in 1702 and was banished to Blois, where she died professing absolute faith in the Roman Catholic Church and its dogmas.

❖ ❖ ❖

Madame Guyon is an early Christian example of a noblewoman putting a life of luxury behind her and publicly propounding a gospel which ran counter to the interests of the Church. Her labors were advertised by the rabid denunciation of clerical authorities, who feared her simple teaching that God is to be found outside as well as inside the Church would put them out of business.

SWEDENBORG

Born 1688—Died 1772 Volume VIII—Page 173

EMINENT SWEDISH THEOLOGIAN

"Swedenborg was cast in heroic mold, and no other man since history began ever compassed in himself so much physical science, and with it all on his back, made such daring voyages into the clouds."—Hubbard.

❖

EMANUEL SWEDENBORG was born in Stockholm and died in London. He was educated at Upsala, and traveled extensively. On his return to Sweden Charles XII made him assessor of mines. He was ennobled in 1719 and the family name changed from Svedberg to Swedenborg. He devoted eleven years to his official duties, framing a systematic description of mining and smelting and the construction of a theory of the origin of creation. His course of life was deflected in 1745, when he professed to have his spiritual senses opened. His recorded experience was unique in that it did not consist in having communication with spirits, but in being himself consciously an inhabitant of the spirit world as if he had died, and thence in associating with the people of that world as one of them. In 1749 he made his first public appearance in his new character in a work entitled *Arcana Cœlesta*, completed in 1756. It is a revelation of the internal, or spiritual, sense of Genesis and Exodus. The chief and distinctive principle of Swedenborgian theology, next to the doctrine of the divine humanity, is the doctrine of life. God alone lives. Creation is dead—man is dead; and their apparent life is the divine presence. Hell as a whole is called the devil, or Satan; there is no supreme individual bearing that name. Swedenborg wrote his works in Latin and received little attention from contemporaries.

❖ ❖ ❖

Swedenborg combined in himself the practical and visionary to an uncommon degree. Having held a most important business post for many years, he suddenly abandoned it for theology, and founded the cult that bears his name. Swedenborg is representative of those who excel in the most opposite undertakings.

VOLTAIRE

Born 1694—Died 1778 Volume VIII—Page 275

THE GREAT FRENCH PHILOSOPHER

"Voltaire sided with the weak, the defenseless, the fallen. . . . His words were a battery that eventually razed the walls of the Bastile, and best of all, freed countless millions from theological superstition, that Bastile of the brain."—Hubbard.

❖

VOLTAIRE, the assumed name of Jean François Marie Arouet, was born and died in Paris. Before graduating from the Collège Louis-le-Grand he began writing poetry. His talents early secured him an introduction into aristocratic French society, but his outspokenness caused him to be twice exiled from Paris between 1716 and 1726, and twice thrown into the Bastile without a trial. Released the second time, he went to England and was there two years before he returned to France and added to his fame as author of the play *Oedipe* by publishing his epic poem on Henry Fourth, *La Henriade*. In 1734 he took up a residence with the Marquise du Châtelet in the Château of Cirey in Lorraine, where he resided until her death in 1749. Subsequently he was for three years the guest of Frederick the Great of Prussia. The visit ended in a quarrel. Exiled from both Prussia and France, Voltaire settled in Geneva, Switzerland, and then at Ferney, a large estate near Geneva, whereon he spent the remainder of his life (1758-78). Much of his time was spent in fighting religious intolerance and fanaticism. Early in 1778, during the reign of Louis XVI, at the request of friends Voltaire determined to visit Paris, where he was received with great enthusiasm. Benjamin Franklin, then living in Paris as agent for the young American Republic, besought Voltaire to bless his grandson, whom he took to call on the Sage of Ferney, a few days before the latter died.

Voltaire is another and notable illustration of the pen being mightier than the sword. Slight and frail in physique, it was solely with a pen that he battled long and valiantly in behalf of all who suffered on account of their religious belief or were victims of political injustice. It is the brain, not the brawn, of a crusader that the Little Journey to Voltaire celebrates.

JOHN WESLEY

Born 1703—Died 1791 Volume IX—Page 11

FOUNDER OF METHODISM

"Wesley was quiet, moderate, conversational, but so earnest that his words carried conviction. The man was honest—he wanted nothing—he gave himself. . . . People were always honored by his presence: even the great and purse-proud, as well as the lowly, welcomed him."—Hubbard.

❖

JOHN WESLEY was born at Epworth, Lincolnshire, England. At ten he was sent to Charterhouse School, and in 1720 he matriculated at Christ Church, Oxford, graduating in 1724. He was ordained deacon in the following year and became a curate to his father in 1727. In 1729 he settled at Oxford, where he became the leader of a band of young men conspicuous for their religious earnestness. They were somewhat derisively called "methodists" from the regularity and strict method of their lives and studies. John Wesley accompanied General Oglethorpe as a missionary to Georgia in 1735, returning to England in 1738. At Savannah he met some of the Moravian brethren, whose simple evangelical piety made a deep impression on him. Presently, however, he abandoned all ecclesiastical traditions and established the Methodist Church. In 1739 he began open-air preaching near Bristol, England, and his success was so pronounced that a special place had to be arranged to take care of the converts. A still more important step was taken in 1740, when the first society was formed under his direction in London. For many years it was the headquarters of Methodism. The first Methodist conference was held in 1744. Wesley preached from twice to four times daily, and traveled (on horseback until advancing age compelled him to use a carriage) about 4,500 miles a year. He died and was buried in the City Road Chapel, London.

❖ ❖ ❖

In the earnestness of his faith and the simplicity of his nature, John Wesley, the founder of Methodism, never imagined what a great and powerful institution was to evolve from his doctrine. All great religious movements have been conceived in the spirit with which Wesley promulgated what has come to be the Methodist Church. In eighteenth century England "no single figure influenced so many minds, no single voice touched so many hearts."

IMMANUEL KANT

Born 1724—Died 1804 **Volume VIII—Page 149**

A GREAT GERMAN METAPHYSICIAN

"*Kant was great enough to doubt appearances and distrust popular conclusions. He knew that fallacies of reasoning follow fast upon actions —reason follows by slow freight. It is quite necessary that we should believe in a Supreme Power, but quite irrelevant that we should prove it.*"—Hubbard.

❖

IMMANUEL KANT, of Scotch descent, was born and died at Königsburg, Prussia. He studied philosophy, mathematics, physics, theology and other subjects at the university of his native town, and took his degree in 1755. In 1770 he became professor of logic and metaphysics at Königsburg, after refusing calls to Erlangen and Jena. In 1778 he had a call to Halle, which he also declined, to remain at his alma mater until his death. Kant's private life was uneventful. He was a bachelor and never traveled. He was austere in his principles of morality, though kindly and courteous in manner, a bold and fearless advocate of political liberty, and a firm believer in human progress. He sympathized with the American Colonies in their struggle with England, and with the French people in their revolt against monarchical abuses. In philosophy he developed slowly. His views did not take final form till he wrote his greatest work, *Critique of Pure Reason*, first published in 1781, in which he endeavors to ascertain the nature of the transcendental ideas of the human understanding and to establish the province of certain human knowledge. His second great work, *Critique of Practical Reason*, appeared in 1788. Finally the third, *Critique of the Power of Judgment*, appeared in 1790. In addition, he published a number of smaller treatises and essays of importance.

Kant represented the type of worker—thinker—who accomplishes more by staying at home than by going away. He used his imagination, instead of his feet, to explore the world, and regarded ordinary "traveling as a fool's paradise." "Kant gained the truth by staying at home," says Hubbard.

FRIEDRICH FROEBEL

Born 1782—Died 1852 Volume X—Page 247

FOUNDER OF THE KINDERGARTEN

"*The same savagery, chilled with fear, that sent Richard Wagner into exile, crushed the life and broke the heart of Friedrich Froebel. . . . Men who govern should be those with a reasonable doubt concerning their own infallibility. We are all children in the Kindergarten of God.*"—Hubbard.

❖

FRIEDRICH WILHELM AUGUST FROEBEL was born at Oberweissbach, in Thuringia, where his father was a Lutheran minister. After a desultory education, including a few months at the University of Jena, he became a school teacher at Frankfort-on-the-Main, and incidentally fell under the influence of Pestalozzi, whose name was the watchword of the Frankfort School. Froebel spent some time with Pestalozzi at Yverdon before entering the German army as a volunteer in 1815. At the close of the Napoleonic wars he devoted himself to the promotion of education, and in 1816 he founded a school at Greisheim called the Universal German Educational Institute. During the next thirty-six years his life work was accomplished. In 1826 he published his most important book *Education of Man*, which is a sort of cornerstone in his philosophy of education. Notwithstanding its comprehensive title, it really discusses the education of a child. The Institute awakened suspicion, and finally opposition, on the part of conservative governments, and the Prince of Schwarzburg-Rudolstadt caused an official inspection of it to be made. The report was favorable, but the work did not gain headway until 1835-6. Even thereafter the kindergarten system had a precarious existence and was banned in Prussia until 1860, long after Froebel's death.

To Froebel a Little Journey is made to illustrate the difficulty and danger that the worker for the advancement of civilization so frequently encounters. For originating the Kindergarten system of education Froebel was scourged in his lifetime, to be rewarded by the gratitude of posterity.

SCHOPENHAUER

Born 1788—Died 1860 Volume VIII—Page 363

Chief Expounder of Pessimism

"Schopenhauer, when asked what kind of people the Berliners were, replied, 'Mostly fools!' 'I believe,' ventured the interrogator—'I believe, Herr Schopenhauer, that you yourself live at Berlin?' 'I do,' was the response, 'and I feel very much at home there.'"—Hubbard.

ARTHUR SCHOPENHAUER was born at Danzig and died at Frankfort-on-the-Main, Germany. His father, a wealthy banker-merchant, planned a business career for him, and with this end in view placed him, in 1805, in the office of a merchant in Hamburg. A few months later his father died, and as soon as the future philosopher became of age he gave up the idea of a business career, and studied first in Göttingen and then in Berlin and Jena. In 1813 he took his degree at the University of Jena on the since celebrated thesis, *On the Fourfold Root of the Principle of Sufficient Reason.* In this treatise he distinguished between the principles of being, of becoming, of knowing and of acting. Part of that year he spent at Weimar, in the company of Goethe, devoting himself to studies in Oriental philosophy and in the theory of color. From 1814 to 1818 he lived in Dresden, occupied in writing a treatise on optics. His principal work, *The World as Will and Idea,* appeared in 1819. He afterwards traveled in Italy, and in 1820 returned to lecture in Berlin in competition with Hegel, who was most popular at the time. Failing to attract a satisfactory audience, Schopenhauer went back to Italy and spent three years there. Again he attempted to displace Hegel in Berlin, but in 1831 retired to Frankfort, where he spent his last years in morose seclusion.

Schopenhauer, being a confirmed pessimist, was always happiest when most miserable, for then, to quote Hubbard, "were his theories proved." Expecting nothing of value, nothing worth having, from the world, the Schopenhauer type of person is agreeably disappointed to be able to live at all.

THOMAS ARNOLD

Born 1795—Died 1842 Volume X—Page 219

A GREAT ENGLISH SCHOOLMASTER

"*The credential of Thomas Arnold to immortality . . . lies in the fact that he fought for a wider horizon in life through education. He lifted his voice for liberty. He believed in the divinity of the child, not in its depravity.*"—Hubbard.

❖

THOMAS ARNOLD, father of Matthew Arnold and best known as the master of Rugby, was born at West Cowes, Isle of Wight, where his father was collector of customs. Graduating from the public schools, he entered Oxford at sixteen and became intimate with John Keble, originator of the Tractarian movement and author of the *Christian Year*, and of John Taylor Coleridge, afterwards Lord Chief Justice of England, by whom he was greatly influenced. He took deacon's orders in 1818, and spent eight years in study and in tutoring. He devoted much attention to Church and social problems that brought upon him fierce attacks in later years. He succeeded to the headmastership of Rugby in 1827, took priestly orders and proceeded to the degrees of B. D. and D. D. The remaining fourteen years of his life were spent at Rugby and at Fox How in Westmoreland, an estate which he bought in 1832. Dr. Percival, who succeeded Arnold at Rugby (1887-95), and who afterwards was Bishop of Hereford, has described him as "a great prophet among schoolmasters." Above all, without its "accredited phraseology of piety," Arnold emphasized the moral and spiritual interest. True scholarship he held to be associated with Christianity. His chief claim to remembrance rests upon his noble life and character.

Thomas Arnold is an excellent example of the right man in the right place. If, as Hubbard says in the Little Journey to the famous headmaster of Rugby, Arnold "had been just a little bigger, the world probably would never have heard of him, for an interdict would have been placed upon his work. The miracle is that, as it was, the Church and State did not snuff him out."

AUGUSTE COMTE

Born 1798—Died 1857 Volume VIII—Page 239

FOUNDER OF POSITIVISM

"Comte's sole claim for immortality lies in the Positive Philosophy, in which he believed he was stating a final truth; to wit: that which is good here is good everywhere, and if there is a future life, the best preparation for it is to live now and here, up to your highest and best."—Hubbard.

❖

ISIDORE AUGUSTE MARIE FRANÇOIS XAVIER COMTE was born at Montpellier, France, and educated at the Ecolé Polytechnique in Paris, from which he was expelled along with other students who revolted against an instructor. From 1816 he supported himself by tutoring. In 1825 he made an unhappy marriage. In the following year he began a course of lectures on his system of philosophy which won the applause of such men as Humboldt and Bainville. Overwork told on him, and after the third lecture he became insane, was placed in an asylum, and attempted suicide. On his mental recovery he became an examiner for entrance to the Ecolé Polytechnique, a post which he held for ten years, after which he was largely supported by his pupils and admirers. John Stuart Mill, with whom Comte had long corresponded, headed a subscription list in England which yielded the French philisopher a substantial sum, and in 1848 a public subscription was so successful as to provide for him thereafter. Meanwhile Comte met Clotilde de Vaux, whose husband was serving a life sentence in prison, and conceived an extravagant affection and admiration for her. The relation, which seems to have been platonic, was broken off by her death a year later, after which Comte had a second mental attack. Of his chief work, *Cours de philosophie positive*, Harriet Martineau made a condensed English translation, approved by the author, in 1853.

The Little Journey to Comte illustrates the highly civilized man who is better at guiding and advising other people than he is at helping himself. Comte regarded himself as the founder of a new religion to save humanity, but twice he suffered mental collapse and was always on the verge of financial bankruptcy.

THEODORE PARKER

Born 1810—Died 1860 Volume IX—Page 275

AN AMERICAN REFORMER

"Theodore Parker was the first of his kind in America—an independent, singlehanded, theological fighter—a preacher without a denomination, dictated to by no bishop, governed by no machine. He has had many imitators, and a few successors."—Hubbard.

❖

THEODORE PARKER was born in Lexington, Massachusetts, and died in Florence, Italy, where his grave is in the Protestant cemetery. He entered Harvard in 1830, and took the full course of study privately, passing all the examinations, but getting no degree because he had paid no tuition fees. Subsequently the degree of M. A. was given him. In 1836 he graduated from the Harvard Divinity School, and in the following year was installed pastor of the West Roxbury Unitarian Church. In 1841 he delivered an ordination sermon, *The Transient and Permanent in Christianity*, which is accounted an epoch-making sermon of the Unitarian development. In 1846 the Twenty-eighth Congregational Society was formed in Boston and he became its minister, preaching to immense congregations for many years. He had inherited a tendency to consumption, and in 1859 was forced to seek a milder climate. He was taken to Santa Cruz, and there wrote his *Experience as a Minister*. From Santa Cruz he went to England and passed his last days in Italy. His Christianity was anti-supernatural; his philosophy intuitional, transcendental; his theology theistic, affirming God, the moral law and immortality as certainties of consciousness. He was one of the most conspicuous leaders of the New England abolitionists.

❖ ❖ ❖

Theodore Parker greatly attracted Hubbard as a minister of the gospel who recognized nothing supernatural in Christianity. Charged with being an infidel, Parker stood his ground and successfully defied the orthodox church to expel him. To quote from the Little Journey, "He drew immense audiences, not because he pandered to the many, but because he deferred to none. . . . He spoke with an inward self-reliance, up to that time, unknown in a single pulpit of America."

HENRY D. THOREAU

Born 1817—Died 1862 Volume VIII—Page 393

AN AMERICAN NATURALIST-PHILOSOPHER

"Henry David Thoreau's place in the common heart of humanity grows firmer and more secure as the seasons pass; his life proves for us again the paradoxical fact that the only men who really succeed are those who fail."—Hubbard.

❖

HENRY DAVID THOREAU, of French and Scotch extraction, was born and died at Concord, Massachusetts, where his father was a manufacturer of lead pencils. At this trade the younger Thoreau worked at intervals. He graduated from Harvard in 1837, and was for some years engaged in school teaching and tutoring at Concord and on Staten Island, N. Y. Deciding to live a life of contemplation, he gave up teaching and proceeded, during the rest of his days, to demonstrate how simply and agreeably one might live on next to nothing financially. From 1845 to 1847 he resided in a hut on the shores of Walden Pond, near Concord. There he lived, doing what little work was required to supply the necessaries of life, and devoting most of his time to the study of nature and the society of friends. On leaving Walden Pond he lived with Ralph Waldo Emerson in Concord (1847-8), and passed the remainder of his life, after 1849, with his parents and sister at Concord. He supported himself by odd jobs of gardening, land surveying, carpentering, etc., without more exertion than was needed to keep him clothed and fed. His large amount of leisure to the time of his death he devoted to the study of nature, to the reading of Greek, Latin, French and English classical literature, to excursions, to pondering metaphysical problems, and to friendly chat with his neighbors, by whom he was beloved.

❖ ❖ ❖

Having once succeeded in making a perfect lead-pencil, Thoreau never made another one, but turned his thoughts to accomplishing other things perfectly. One of them, which Hubbard dwells upon in the Little Journey, was to prove that most worldly possessions are encumbrances and are not necessary to the proper conduct of life.

HERBERT SPENCER

Born 1820—Died 1903 Volume VIII—Page 325

FOUNDER OF SYNTHETIC PHILOSOPHY

"Herbert Spencer's work was all a matter of analytical demonstration. And while the word 'materialist' was everywhere applied to him, and he did not resent it, yet he was one of the most spiritual of men."—Hubbard.

❖

HERBERT SPENCER was born at Derby, and died at Brighton, England. He was articled as a civil engineer in 1837, but in 1845 abandoned engineering in favor of literature. He was assistant editor of the *Economist* (1848-53), and in 1855 (four years before the appearance of Darwin's *Origin of Species*) he published his *Principles of Psychology*, which is based on the principle of evolution. In 1860 he issued a prospectus of his *System of Synthetic Philosophy*, in which, beginning with the first principles of knowledge, he proposed to trace the progress of evolution in life, mind, society and morality. It met with a disappointing reception, and the work would have been abandoned but for the timely aid of American friends, headed by Professor E. L. Youmans of Yale, founder of *Popular Science Monthly*, whereby he was enabled to proceed. Over-application had some time since brought on a serious attack of nervous prostration, which obliged Spencer for the rest of his life to shorten his working hours. He became a chronic sufferer from dyspepsia and insomnia. His health was especially precarious in the early 60's and it was a question as to whether he would live to complete his great work, which, however, was done in 1880. It consists of *First Principles* (1862); *Principles of Biology* (1864); *Principles of Psychology* (1871-2); *Principles of Sociology* (1876-80); *Principles of Ethics* (1879).

It is because Herbert Spencer propounded the sanest, most intelligible and convincing system of philosophy ever conceived, that a Little Journey is made to him. Hubbard observes that no one could meet Spencer without being impressed with the fact that he was in the presence of a most superior person. The Little Journey to Spencer reminds us that everyone automatically advertises what he does and thinks.

MARY BAKER EDDY

Born 1821—Died 1910 Volume X—Page 329

DISCOVERER AND FOUNDER OF CHRISTIAN SCIENCE

"*The valuable truths and distinguishing features of Christian Science are not to be found in Mrs. Eddy's books, but in Mrs. Eddy's life. She was a much bigger woman than she was a writer . . . Christian Science is as yet the lengthened shadow of Mary Baker Eddy.*"—Hubbard.

❖

MARY BAKER EDDY (at first Mary Baker) was born at Bow, near Concord, New Hampshire. Her immediate family were people of considerable prominence and prosperity, and her ancestry was distinguished. Her parents were members of the Congregational Church. One of her tutors was the Reverend Enoch Corser, a Congregational minister, who regarded her at the age of fifteen as "an intellectual and spiritual genius." From her childhood until more than a decade after her discovery of Christian Science Mrs. Eddy was a Congregationalist. She was married three times: first to Major George W. Glover, in 1843. Left a widow within a year, in 1853 she married Dr. Daniel S. Patterson, a dentist. In 1873, after her removal to Lynn, Mass., and her discovery of Christian Science, she divorced him, and in 1877 married Asa Gilbert Eddy, the first of her students to engage in the practice of Christian Science healing. He died in 1882, after having helped to sustain Mrs. Eddy during the period in which the Church of Christ, Scientist, was organized and the movement encountered its first active opposition. Her first church was organized in Boston in 1879, and she opened the Massachusetts Metaphysical College there in 1881. The first edition of her *Science and Health, with Key to the Scriptures,* was published in 1875 at her own expense. She was the active leader of the movement she instituted until her decease.

Hubbard makes a Little Journey to Mary Baker Eddy as a woman who had great faith in herself, hence in others; great knowledge of the strength and weakness of human nature; and who had extraordinary ability to exploit and apply her gospel beneficially as well as profitably.

INDEX

❖

INDEX

INDEX